THE FOG OF WAR

MARTHA GELLHORN AT THE D-DAY LANDINGS

A FEARLESS JOURNALIST ON A PERILOUS JOURNEY

Michelle Jabès Corpora is an American author who has ghostwritten five novels in a world-famous, bestselling mystery series. She is also the author of *American Horse Tales: The Dust Bowl* (Penguin Workshop). She spends her time learning about history, working on political campaigns, and practicing Brazilian jiu-jitsu. Michelle lives in Maryland with her husband, two daughters, a pair of long-haired guinea pigs, and a calico cat.

THE FOG OF WAR

MARTHA GELLHORN AT THE D-DAY LANDINGS

MICHELLE JABÈS CORPORA
With illustrations by Amerigo Pinelli

PUSHKIN CHILDREN'S

Pushkin Press
71–75 Shelton Street
London WC2H 9JQ

First published in the UK by Pushkin Press in 2021

1 3 5 7 9 8 6 4 2

ISBN 13: 978-1-78269-313-0

Designed and typeset by Tetragon, London
Printed and bound by CPI Group (UK) Ltd, Croydon, CRO 4YY

www.pushkinpress.com

1

A MAN'S JOB

It was morning in March 1944, and Martha Gellhorn stood on the patio of her house in Havana, Cuba, her bare feet pressed against the cool stone tiles. She looked out over the big ceiba tree, which looked like a child had drawn it, and over the distant palms to the sea beyond. A breeze that smelled of salt and flowers swept her blonde hair back over her shoulders.

She breathed it all in, the bright freshness of the morning washing away the last shreds of sleep. Cuba was always beautiful. Martha sighed. *One could almost forget that there's a war going on*, she thought. *Two wars, in fact.*

One of them, World War Two, was reaching fever pitch. It was almost impossible to keep up with all of the troop movements and battles and bombings, even for a seasoned war correspondent like Martha. She had spent the last five months in Europe, writing more than two dozen articles about the War for *Collier's*. She fed the weekly US magazine thousands upon thousands of words, but it remained ever hungry for more. And Martha knew that the biggest story of all was still yet to come: the invasion of France across the English Channel. No one knew exactly when, of course – that was top secret. But if the Allied forces were able to retake Western Europe from the Nazis, then it would turn the tide in their favour.

Any day now, *Collier's* would send word that she'd be the one receiving the accreditation to report on the invasion. Only one reporter per magazine was allowed, and she was certain she was going to be chosen. She was their most decorated war correspondent, after all. But in the past few days, she'd begun to worry about getting back to London in time. She gripped the metal railing of the patio, the sharp corners biting into her palms. *I never should have left*, she thought. Cuba was beautiful all right, and a welcome sight after war-torn Europe, but it wasn't where she belonged. For all the sunshine and flowers and quiet solitude, her home in Havana was the battlefield for the other war going on.

The war with her husband, Ernest Hemingway.

At first, it had been terribly exciting being married to the most famous writer in the world. They fell in love on the battlefields of Spain, and spent their first years together leaping from one great adventure to the next. War and words had brought them together, but now they seemed to be tearing them apart. Now that they were married, Ernest no longer seemed to admire Martha's commitment to her work. In fact, he hated it. *Are you a war correspondent*, he'd written in one of his cables, *or wife?* Martha didn't understand why she couldn't be both.

His letters had followed her across Europe, full of complaints and bitterness about her absence. She tried her best to soothe him in her replies. She called him her 'beloved Bug', and pleaded with him to join her overseas. But all her letters seemed to do no good. Ernest was as stubborn as a mule, and wouldn't be told what to do. And so, against her better judgement, Martha had come back to the *Finca Vigía*, their house on a hill, hoping to patch things up between them.

She'd told herself it was the right thing to do. It was her duty, she thought, to try and talk some sense into the man, face to face. But her homecoming seemed only to make things worse. They'd fought the moment she arrived back in Cuba, and every day since.

A grey tabby cat slipped out onto the patio and wound around her ankles, snapping Martha out of her thoughts. She bent to pick him up, and he bumped his face against hers. 'Hello, Will,' she said. 'I suppose you want your breakfast?' The warm, purring body of the cat soothed her. *Perhaps today will be better,* she thought, hopeful. *It certainly couldn't be worse.*

As Martha walked down the two flights of steps back to the main floor, other cats appeared, all yowling for attention. Ernest had a soft spot for the little beasts, and let them run amok like they owned the place. 'Yes, yes, darlings,' Martha said, trying to make her way through their winding bodies without falling down the stairs. 'I know you're hungry, so am I. Where's your *Papa*?'

She came to the landing and walked into the living room, to find Ernest sitting bare-chested in one of the squashy armchairs patterned with pink roses. His bushy salt-and-pepper beard was particularly wild this morning, and Martha thought he made quite a picture – this bulldog of a man, scowling at a newspaper, nestled in his pretty flowered chair. Undoubtedly, Ernest would have chosen more manly furniture, something made of leather and mahogany, but Martha had wanted the flowers.

All around Ernest, the house was an unholy mess, as it had been when she'd arrived back. Dirty dishes and clothes were piled up in every room, empty bottles left to gather dust and flies, and a haze of unwashed stink hung over everything.

He hadn't noticed her yet. Martha took a deep breath and entered the room, the legion of cats following close behind. But she'd only made it a few steps before nearly breaking her neck tripping over a bottle of whiskey left on the floor beside the sofa. 'Oh!' Martha cried out in surprise, catching herself before she fell. The bottle tumbled over, its caramel-coloured contents glugging out onto the floor where a pile of books lay scattered.

Ernest looked up over his newspaper, his eyes alighting on the books slowly soaking up whiskey. 'Clumsy woman!' he exclaimed, jumping up from his chair to rescue them. He brushed off the covers with one hand, and shook his head in dismay. 'This one's a first edition too.'

'If you care so much for your books,' Martha muttered, grabbing a ragged undershirt and using it to mop up the puddle of liquor, 'perhaps you'd think to put them back on the shelf where they belong.'

'*Perhaps* if you were a proper wife and did a little cleaning once in a while,' Ernest snapped back, 'I wouldn't need to.' He turned to the cats. 'Come on now, cotsies, Papa will feed you.' The cats piled after him to the kitchen, a colourful, meowing ocean of fur.

Martha's face grew hot, and she felt the fire of rage rekindling in her chest. 'Good morning to you, too,' she muttered into the empty room. He'd made this mess, she fumed. Why should she clean it up? Why was his work so much more important than hers?

Her hopes of a better day vanished. *No*, she thought grimly. *Today promises to be quite as dreadful as all the rest*.

The smell of hot coffee reached her, and she walked into the dining room to pour herself a cup from the steaming silver pot Ernest had left on the table. The bittersweet taste cleared her mind a little. She sat down in one of the wooden chairs with her cup, the open French doors letting in that same fragrant breeze from the garden. The room was spare and white, one wall made up only of windows, and the other lined with the mounted heads of animals Ernest had killed on safari in Africa. *It's no use staying here*, she thought. *Ernest has dug his heels in, and nothing I can say or do will change his mind. It's time I started planning my return to Europe. I'll call my editor at* Collier's *at once and discuss my accreditation*.

Her decision was made. The little war at home could no longer distract her from the real one. Now came the hard part: breaking the news to her husband.

'Ernest,' she called out. 'Listen, we need to talk.'

The racket in the kitchen stopped, and a few moments later Ernest appeared in the doorway, a wolfish smile on his face.

'You're right, we do.'

Martha's body tensed. She had expected to have the upper hand, but something about Ernest's expression set off alarm bells in her mind. It was a red cape at a bullfight, bait on a hook. It taunted her, waiting for her to bite.

'Well,' Martha went on, determined not to be rattled. 'I think you'd agree that my coming home hasn't solved a thing. And each day that passes is a day closer to the invasion. I need to be there, Ernest. For *Collier's*, and for myself. So I'm going.'

She held her breath. She thought he would stomp and shout and throw things, as he usually did when she put her foot down. But instead, his smile only broadened.

'I'm afraid you'll find that job is already taken,' he said.

Martha's blood turned to ice. 'What do you mean?'

'I mean *Collier's* gave their accreditation to me,' Ernest replied. 'An honour I am proud to accept.'

Martha felt like she'd been slapped. 'But – how? What?' she sputtered, her mind spinning.

'It's simple, really,' Ernest continued. 'I agreed to write about the brave Royal Air Force pilots, so Mr Dahl at the embassy in Washington has fixed me up with a plane seat to London. Hard to come by opportunities like that nowadays, wouldn't you agree? No ladies allowed on board, though. Shame.'

Martha's hands were balled into fists, her breath coming in short bursts as her whole body filled up like a balloon with helpless rage. 'How could you?' she said through gritted teeth. 'How could you go behind my back and betray me? Take away the one thing you *know* I—'

Ernest squinted at her, tilting his head. 'Betray you?' he said, his voice sweet but cruel. 'But, darling, isn't this exactly what you wanted?'

Martha carefully set down her cup of coffee so she wouldn't throw it at him. It was true: Martha had suggested some months ago that he write for *Collier's*. She'd even been the one to arrange the connection with Roald Dahl at the British embassy. But she'd only done that as a kindness, in hopes of getting him to join her at the front. She never dreamed that Ernest would use it as a chance to take her place.

'You *knew* they would choose you over me,' she said, pointing an accusing finger at him. 'You knew that no matter how much work I'd done, no matter how many articles I'd written, they'd toss me aside for the *great* Ernest Hemingway. Don't deny it.'

Ernest walked over to the table and picked up the coffee cup she'd set down, draining it in one gulp. 'Why would I?' he said, licking his lips. 'It's true. Why would they pick a woman for a man's job?' He placed the cup back in front of her, empty, and turned to leave. 'I'll be getting my affairs in order and leaving for New York as soon as possible,' he called back to her. 'You'll make sure the cats are taken care

of while I'm away, won't you? And for God's sake, do something about this mess.'

Martha stood frozen in the middle of the room, listening first to footsteps in the hallway, and then to the sound of Ernest rattling around in the bedroom, probably pulling down suitcases and his typewriter from the shelves.

It took all of her willpower not to scream. Not to smash every beautiful thing in this home that she'd loved, this place that was being transformed into a prison.

She raised her gaze to the antelope head mounted on the wall in front of her. It stared back with glassy eyes, its elegant wildness trapped and mute.

Another one of Ernest's trophies, she thought. *Just like me.*

Martha slammed her fist on the table, overturning the empty coffee cup.

No.

Her anger began to give way to determination. Her heart slowed. One of the cats jumped up onto the table and sniffed her hand, probably curious about all the noise. 'It's all right, love,' she whispered, scratching him behind the ears. 'Everything's going to be all right.'

He can't keep me here, she thought. *He can take my job, but he can't keep me here.*

I'll find a way to London if it's the last thing I do.

CROSSING THE OCEAN

The next few weeks were a whirlwind, but that was OK – Martha liked a whirlwind. She left Cuba as soon as she could, and went to Washington, D.C. where she had an open invitation to stay with her friend, the First Lady, Eleanor Roosevelt. The food at the White House wasn't very good, but the company was.

Martha had been tirelessly working to secure transport to London, but with no success. She felt stuck – but Eleanor, as always, was happy to offer some wise advice. 'Do not be so discouraged,' she told Martha over breakfast one day. 'I have never known you to back down from a fight, and I don't expect you to now. If there's a way to get there, you'll find it.'

After being turned away from what seemed like every boat and plane in the country, Martha's friend,

Alan Grover, finally offered her a place aboard a Norwegian ship leaving from New York. Martha was thrilled.

'Er, yes,' Alan said over the phone. 'There's just one catch.'

'What is it?' Martha asked.

'The voyage will take about three weeks, and you'll be the only passenger aboard. Also, the ship's cargo is mostly explosives.'

'That's three catches, Alan.'

'Sorry, but it's the best I can do.'

'So when the ship is accidentally blown to bits, I'll likely be sharing my final moments with a seagull, is that what you're saying?'

'That's about the size of it.'

Martha sighed. 'All right, I'll take it.'

I suppose if I'm going to go out, she thought as she hung up the phone, *it might as well be with a bang!*

After a warm goodbye to Eleanor and the President, she left for New York City at once.

The weeks aboard the Norwegian ship were some of the loneliest of Martha's life.

It was nice at first, having time to catch up on her reading and writing letters to friends – but that got boring pretty quickly. The showers were short and cold, and the food was tasteless. Martha often just stood up on the deck, staring out at the sea as the massive freighter sliced through the water. She knew that way out beyond the horizon, the symphony of war was marching towards a crescendo. But there on the big empty ship, the silence kept her up at night. She tossed and turned in her thin, hard little cot, thinking about what was to come.

No one but the top brass knew exactly when the invasion was supposed to begin – the whole thing was shrouded in secrecy. Everything Martha had written about the War had been picked over by the censors, and anything with even the faintest whiff of real information had been cut long before it could ever reach the pages of the magazine. But Martha and all the other war correspondents knew the invasion was happening soon. The first week of June, some said. If all went to plan, Martha should arrive in England just in time.

Just in time to do what, exactly?

It was a question that stuck with her, like a piece of food lodged in her teeth. Ernest hadn't been able to keep her at home, true, but he still had her accreditation. Without it, she was barred from the war front. The fact was, she'd been so focused on just making it to London, she hadn't spent any time thinking about what she'd do once she got there.

Patience, she told herself. *One problem at a time.*

For the first week, it was all she could do not to keep fuming about Ernest. *This is all his fault*, she

19

kept thinking. *If it weren't for him, I wouldn't have to worry about any of this.* But the further she travelled from her life back home, the further all that stuff and mess went from her mind. Instead, it was slowly replaced by the thrill she always felt at the beginning of a new assignment. She never cared very much about interviewing the rich and powerful, although she found some of them quite fascinating. What she really looked forward to was being amongst ordinary people. Eating with them, marching beside them, finding out first-hand what it was like to be in their shoes. Those stories were the closest things to pure truth that Martha ever produced.

By the time the coast of England emerged from the darkness early one morning, Martha's anger had evaporated like mist. She'd managed to cross the ocean without losing her mind or being blown to bits, and that felt like a victory. Her pen and notebook were in hand; her typewriter stowed carefully in her suitcase. She was ready to begin.

After twenty days of solitude, Martha's arrival back into the world of people was delightfully noisy. The port of Liverpool was bustling with activity as she walked down the ramp from the ship, her sea legs as shaky as a new-born fawn's. The breeze smelled of iron and petrol, and everywhere were the sounds of shouting and boots clomping along the wooden docks.

Martha blinked into the sunlight, like a bear waking up after a long winter. *Finally!* she thought. *I'm back in the land of the living.* There was a familiar tension in the air, something she'd come to know from her days spent on the front line of so many wars. It was a feeling of expectation, everyone just waiting for something great and terrible to happen. This might have been frightening to most people, but Martha felt electrified with excitement. Strange as it might sound, she always felt most herself when in the midst of such stupendous trouble.

Huge cranes were hoisting crates of equipment high up into the air along the length of the docks, while English sailors in navy-blue uniforms gathered in packs, chatting and laughing together. Meanwhile, American troops dressed in olive-green coats and helmets were disembarking from another ship nearby, weighed down like mules with packs and rifles. Martha raised quite a few eyebrows as she made her way through the crowd, her uncovered head of golden hair like a beacon amongst the sea of green and blue.

She bumped up against an American soldier, whose boyish face lit up with a smile as he turned to see her. 'Well, you're a sight for sore eyes,' he said playfully.

'So are you,' Martha replied, and she was tickled by the surprise on the faces of the soldier and his buddies at her boldness. But before he could get another word in, Martha hurried past them to the street, where she could meet the driver she'd hired to take her to London.

It was impossible to ride through England without seeing constant reminders of the War. Buildings, churches, and homes across Liverpool and Birmingham still sat in sad piles of grey rubble, even though it had been four years since German bombs rained down on them during the Blitz. It was strange to drive through streets of total devastation, while only a block away, other buildings stood untouched. There seemed to be no rhyme or reason to it. In fact, the Germans' main goal of the relentless attacks had been to crush England's spirit as well as their ability to fight. But it hadn't worked – not a bit. Martha watched people walk past ruined buildings, milkmen carrying fresh bottles to leave on doorsteps, mothers pushing prams with children running beside them, men in sharp suits and hats, rolled-up newspapers shoved under their arms. All of them, Martha noticed, walked with their heads held high. She made mental notes of everything she saw – the clothes they wore, the expressions on their faces, the way their backs were so straight despite the heavy weight they carried. This was the fuel for all of Martha's writing about war. Not just facts and figures, but the beating hearts of the people who lived through it.

After a long drive, Martha finally arrived at The Dorchester, the London five-star hotel where many of the other correspondents were staying. The Dorchester was like an alien world, where everything was bright and shining and unbroken, and people smiled as if there was nothing wrong at all.

Martha was standing at the front desk in the lobby, picking up her room key, when she felt a shadow fall over her. She turned to see a man, his head wrapped in bandages, staring at her as if he'd seen a ghost.

'Oh, hello, Ernest,' Martha said lightly. She worked very hard not to smile.

Ernest sputtered, his face changing from white to red to purple, before muttering, 'What are you *doing* here?'

'The same thing you are, of course,' she replied.

Ernest shook his head in disbelief. 'Have you forgotten?' he growled. '*I* have the accreditation. Not you. You're wasting your time, Marty. You came all this way for nothing.'

Martha narrowed her eyes. 'We'll see about that.' She glanced at his bandaged head. 'What happened to you, anyway?' she asked.

Ernest sniffed. 'Car accident.'

Martha tutted. 'Pity. You should save your derring-do for the battlefront. That's what I plan to do.'

'You are delusional, woman,' Ernest chuckled, shaking his head. 'You will never see the battlefront. Go home.'

With that, he turned and walked away, joining a group of other correspondents who welcomed him with open arms. '*Papa!*' they shouted. Martha gritted her teeth, took up her key and made her way to the lifts.

Up in her room, she dropped all of her bags on the bed and set up her typewriter on the desk by the window. Her fingers drifted across the keys. She was tired, but too agitated by her run-in with Ernest to take any rest. She'd told him she'd make it to the battlefront – but how? Maybe one of the other correspondents could help. Maybe she should take it up with one of her military connections.

Maybe, maybe…

Over the next few days, Martha tried everything she could think of. But it seemed that the military gentlemen had no time for her, and the other correspondents were too busy partying to help anyone.

Martha's friends urged her to join them, but she simply couldn't bear the long, loud parties. It wasn't that she blamed them for wanting to have fun. She understood how important that was at a time like this. When she'd visited an English bomber station seven months earlier, every free night the soldiers had flocked to the village nearby to dance at the hall and watch old movies. It made sense to take the good times when you could. How else could you make it through?

No, Martha couldn't bring herself to party because she was too consumed with the problem of her accreditation. Time was running out, and she still didn't have a plan.

Word spread that the invasion of France – D-Day – was set for the 5th of June. But when the morning came, Martha could see right away it was not a good day. Heavy clouds hung in the sky outside her window, and a blustery wind blew hats off the men in the street as they made their way to work through the pouring rain. *Not exactly the weather you want for the largest seaborne invasion in history*, she thought. *They'll have no choice but to push it back until tomorrow.*

That night, there were no more parties. Everyone in the hotel, everyone in the country, really – seemed to be holding their breath.

Martha was fast asleep when there was a sharp rapping at her hotel room door. She woke up with a groan. The room was still dark, with only a few weak rays of sunlight filtering through the curtains. She glanced with one eye at her bedside clock – it was a little before 6.00 a.m.

'What?' she called, her voice still thick with sleep.

The head of a uniformed airman popped through the door, letting a cascade of warm yellow light from the hallway spill inside. 'Just letting you know, Miss Gellhorn – it's happening.'

The words didn't really register in Martha's brain. 'Don't be silly,' she mumbled. 'Waking me up early like this, it's simply—'

'No, really,' the airman broke in. 'They're all gathering in the press room. It's happening.'

Martha blinked as his message finally sunk in. Suddenly she was very much awake. 'I asked you to do this, didn't I?' she said.

'Yes, ma'am,' the airman replied. 'No matter what hour, you said.'

Martha nodded, the memory finally returning. 'Of course I did. Thank you, airman.'

And with that, he shut the door and was gone.

Martha sat up in bed, and turned to the window. Outside, the sky was the colour of iron. But there was no rain.

The invasion, she thought, dread and excitement mingling within her. *D-Day. It's today.*

IT'S HAPPENING!

This must be what a rat in a cage feels like.

It was later that morning, and Martha sat locked in the press room with the other correspondents who had been left behind. She was stuck between one reporter who banged on his portable typewriter so fast that it made her head hurt, and another one who was so nervous that he could barely hold onto his cup of coffee without spilling it. His hands trembled as he set it down in its saucer, making a sound like teeth chattering.

Outside, she could hear the distant, deep growl of bomber planes flying overhead. She gritted her teeth. To be sitting in this room, and not out *there* ... it was pure torture.

After what seemed like an eternity, the doors were opened again. *Finally!* Martha thought, relieved, and hurried out. She might not have thought of a way to reach the battlefront yet, but she wasn't one to waste precious time. She took a taxi to Westminster Abbey, and spent hours out in the freezing cold talking to soldiers and passers-by, getting comments and reactions about the War. She tried to concentrate on the people, but she was distracted, haunted by questions.

Had the Allies' plan worked? Was the invasion going well?

Where's Ernest? Is he safe? Or did he do something dreadfully brave and stupid and get himself killed?

You worked so hard to be here today, Martha Gellhorn, what are you doing now that you're here?

After a few hours, Martha felt her determination falter. She put away her pen and her notebook in her handbag, and just started to walk.

The streets of London were cold and empty. She shivered as a chill breeze blew down Constitution Hill, rustling the green trees that lined the street. *Shhh*, the trees said needlessly. The whole city was already as quiet as a mouse.

Soon she found herself at the black and gold gates of Buckingham Palace. Even the Queen's house was still, with only a few soldiers and official-looking men going in and out. Everyone, it seemed, was huddled indoors – just waiting.

Martha continued on into St James's Park, turning onto a footpath along the lake. The ducks didn't seem to be bothered by the War, and gathered in teams on the water, diving for fish. Martha was about to find a place to sit and watch them when she spotted a yellow handkerchief on the grass. She picked it up, and saw that it had the initials *EP* embroidered in blue at the corner. Looking around, she saw a woman sitting on a park bench nearby.

'Excuse me,' Martha said, walking over to her. 'Is this yours?'

The woman looked up at Martha through a pair of thick glasses. She had a round face and chestnut-brown skin, and wore a black hat with a felted red poppy pinned to it. Looking down at the yellow handkerchief, she nodded. 'That's mine, all right,' she said, taking it and tucking it into her coat. 'Thanks very much.'

'Edith, is it?' Martha said, sitting down next to her on the bench.

The woman's eyes narrowed. 'Now, how did you know that?' she asked, her voice laced with suspicion.

'Your handkerchief,' Martha said. '*EP*. You look about my age, and there were a lot of Ediths about when I was in school. Just a wild guess, really.'

'Goodness, I thought you were some kind of government spy!' Edith said, shaking her head in amazement. She stuck her hand out to Martha. 'I'm called Edith, all right. Edith Prince.'

Martha grasped her hand and gave it a hearty shake. 'Martha Gellhorn. Pleasure to meet you, Edith. And no, I'm hardly a spy – just a nosy journalist.' She sighed. 'Although right now, I'm hardly even that any more.'

'What do you mean?' Edith asked.

Martha frowned. 'Well, I *should* be reporting on the battlefront, but my husband took my spot.'

'So what?' Edith replied. 'Take it back.'

Martha laughed. 'Oh, believe me, I tried. You don't know my husband. He always gets what he wants.'

'Hmm,' Edith replied. Then she grimaced, and reached down to pull off one of her black Oxford shoes. She turned it upside down and shook it, and a shower of sand fell out. 'Bloomin' sand gets into everything,' she muttered.

Martha was puzzled. 'Sand?'

Edith nodded and pulled the shoe back on. 'I'm a firewatcher. When you sign up for the job, you get a bucket of sand, a bucket for water and a little hand pump. Been doing it for months. There's probably sand in my ears by now!'

A firewatcher! Martha thought. She'd heard of them before. When they weren't working their everyday jobs, firewatchers would take turns standing on top of buildings during the raids to watch out for firebombs. German planes would drop hundreds of them at a time, and the firewatchers were supposed to find where the bombs landed and use the sand and water to snuff out the flames. 'That's quite a dangerous job,' she said to Edith.

Edith shrugged. 'It's a doddle, really,' she said. 'I thought if the boys can go out there and fight the Nazis, then I can handle a few fires. I'm a member of the Commonwealth, I'm meant to do whatever I can to protect it.' She looked back at the ducks in the lake. They'd floated closer and were making curious quacking noises, probably hoping to be tossed a few crumbs. 'I like coming here to watch the ducks, because no matter what's going on, they're here, doing their thing. They swim, they preen, they eat fish. There can be bombs falling all around them and they're still here. You know what I mean? The ducks don't let anything stop them from being ducks. It's a good way to live, don't you think?'

The two women fell into silence, and Martha thought about what Edith had said. Here she was, feeling like Ernest had stolen something vital, as if she was nothing without her accreditation. *You're the same woman you were before*, she told herself. *And Martha Gellhorn always finds a way. He can't take that from you.*

She'd let herself give up. And that wasn't Ernest's fault. It was hers. She stood up suddenly.

'Going somewhere?' Edith asked.

'Yes,' Martha answered. 'I'm going where I should have gone in the first place.' She started to make her way back to the path, but turned back and called out: 'Thank you, Edith! Those firebombs don't stand a chance against you!'

Martha broke into a run down the paths of the park until she reached a main road. From there, she waved down a black cab and hopped into the back seat.

'Where to, miss?' the driver asked.

'Southampton port, please,' Martha replied. 'I need to get to the docks right away! There's a big tip in it for you if you floor it.'

Less than two hours later, the black cab pulled up to a street corner near the docks of Southampton. 'You sure this is where you want to go, miss?' the driver asked, eyeing the crowds of soldiers and officers that filled the port.

'I'm sure,' Martha said, grabbing a fistful of notes from her bag and handing it over. 'Thanks very much!' she said gaily, and stepped out onto the street.

The grey sky was unchanged from the morning, though it was early evening now. Martha immediately melted into the crowd, heading towards the ships waiting to leave for France. They sat heavy in the water, dull grey or camouflaged, much like the men themselves. Soldiers swarmed onto them like ants, and Martha spied tanks and all manner of other equipment already loaded onto their crowded decks.

Her plan was simple: find a ship going to the front, and board it. Figuring out how to actually do that? Well, that was the tricky part.

This might be harder than I thought, Martha mused, glancing at all the military personnel. *I'd stick out like a sore thumb. They'd toss me off before we left the docks.* She felt wild with impatience. She was so close! There had to be a way—

Suddenly she felt a hand on her shoulder. 'Excuse me, ma'am,' said a voice. 'May I ask what you're doing here?'

Martha steadied her breath and turned around to see a military policeman standing before her. He was young, and his uniform looked a little bit too big for him, which only made him look younger. Seeing an opportunity, Martha smiled her winningest smile. 'Yes, of course, officer,' she replied smoothly, and pulled out an old press pass to show him. 'I'm a correspondent for *Collier's*, the American magazine. I'm sure you've heard of it?'

The policeman stood up a little straighter. 'Um, yes – of course I have,' he said. 'What of it?'

'Yes, well…' Martha said, scanning the docks behind him for an idea, any idea. And then her eyes landed upon an enormous white ship, like a swan among crows. It had a green stripe running along its side, and big red crosses painted along its hull. *A hospital ship!* she thought. *That's perfect!* 'I am here to interview the nurses on that medical ship there,' she continued, hardly missing a beat. 'To get a woman's perspective, you understand. It's good you've found me, officer. I'd so appreciate your help getting on board.'

The policeman's face lit up at the mention of him being helpful, and he quite happily parted the crowd to allow Martha to pass through. He even waved at her as she boarded the vessel. She waved back, and then ducked inside.

Remarkably, no one questioned her as she walked through the main deck. They were all too concerned with their own duties, and anyway, Martha knew to walk with purpose. *Just act like you belong*, she told herself. *Look like you have somewhere to go.*

But she had no idea where she was going. At least, until she passed by a tiny ship's lavatory, which was no larger than a store cupboard. Without a second thought, she stepped into the room, shut the door behind her and locked it tight. The fading light of day streamed through a tiny porthole in one wall, and through it, she could still hear the muted buzz of activity from the port.

Martha sat down on the toilet seat and grinned like a fox, her heart hammering.

By God, she thought, *I've done it!*

STOWAWAY

Hours went by. Martha watched all the light disappear from the horizon through the little porthole, and passed the time by counting the tiles on the lavatory floor. At one point she dozed off, and awoke later with a crick in her neck. She got up from where she'd been sitting, turned on the tap in the tiny sink, and splashed some cold water on her face. She stared at her reflection in the small mirror. *Well, you got what you wanted*, a voice in her head piped up. *You lied to a police officer, broke a few laws and snuck onto a military vessel to do it, but here you are.*

Martha grimaced. *I had to do those things to be able to do my job*, she shot back at the annoying voice. *A duck can't stop being a duck, and I can't stop being a war correspondent. Especially not because of some ungrateful magazine editors, stupid rules and my Ernest's enormous ego. I did what I did, and I won't be sorry for it.*

That shut the voice up quite nicely. Martha smiled at herself in the mirror, and took a moment to powder her nose.

Then, a moment later, the doorknob to the lavatory rattled. Martha stood completely still, not even daring to breathe. It rattled again, and a man's voice called out, 'Oi! Anyone in there?'

Martha's mind spun. If she said nothing, then he might think the door was jammed and try to break it open. 'Er, yes,' she sputtered. 'I'm not feeling too well, I'll need a few minutes…'

'Oh!' the man replied, probably a little surprised at the sound of a woman's voice. 'Of course, miss, I'll come back later.' Martha listened to his footsteps and then heard him stop to talk to someone else. 'Don't bother with that one, James,' he said. 'Lady's in there, probably one of them American nurses. Sick as a dog and we haven't even left the docks yet! God help her when we cross the Channel…' The two men chuckled and went on their way.

Martha let out a sigh of relief, and sagged down to her spot in the corner. *Whew! I'm safe – for now at least.* She reached into her bag for a lemon drop, popped one into her mouth and closed her eyes to wait.

Finally, sometime after midnight, she felt the ship's engines rumble to life beneath her. It seemed to take an eternity for them to pull away from the harbour, but finally they were out on the open water. Martha stood up and brushed a few flecks of dirt from her coat. *Time to get out there*, she thought. *It's not like they're going to throw me overboard now, even if I do get caught.* She took a deep breath, unlocked the lavatory door, and stepped out into the dimly lit passageway. There was no one around, although she could hear voices through the bulkheads. She took a few careful steps forwards, and spied a door marked 'SUPPLY' next to the lavatory. Curious, she eased open the door and peeked inside. In addition to some medical masks and gowns and a pile of thin grey blankets, there were a couple of nurse's uniforms folded neatly on a shelf. They were army green, and came with white armbands emblazoned with a red cross.

Bingo.

With a smile, Martha grabbed one and a set of boots, and hurried back to the lavatory to change. Stuffing her old clothes into a corner, she pulled on the rough trousers and jacket. She caught sight of herself in the mirror and pulled her hair up into a bun at the nape of her neck. *Can't be going off to war looking a mess, now can I?* she thought.

A few minutes later, Martha was walking down the passageway once more, dressed in full uniform. She adjusted the army-green beret on her head, and felt for the tiny notebook and pen she'd slipped into the pocket of her trousers. She wouldn't be able to take too many notes without raising suspicion, but hopefully she'd have a chance to scribble a few words down. *Well*, she thought. *Here goes nothing.*

Hearing women's voices ahead, she peeked into a long room full of dozens and dozens of bunk beds. Their metal frames were suspended overhead by chains, like hanging potted plants, one above another, so that they'd be able to fit two patients into one small space. Huge rolls of bandages were stacked against one bulkhead, along with shelves full of medicine bottles of all kinds. There were three women there, all dressed in uniforms just like Martha's. Two were busy checking that all the supplies were in order, and the third was sitting on one of the lower bunks, staring out the porthole at the inky black world beyond.

'Hey, Lizzie,' said one of the busy ones. She had dark, curly hair that spilled out from under her beret, and spoke with a heavy Texas accent. 'I reckon we could use a hand over here.'

Lizzie took a deep breath. She was fair-skinned and tall, her light brown hair pulled into a ponytail. 'It was supposed to be a train!' she finally said.

The other two nurses looked at each other. 'What?' the third one said. Her freckled face was a mask of confusion.

39

'Back at training,' Lizzie replied. 'They said that we'd be caring for the wounded on a *train*. Not a boat! I can't work like this – I get seasick!' It was only then that Martha noticed Lizzie's skin was a pale shade of green.

'Oh, honey, you're just nervous,' the curly-haired Texan said. 'This ain't my first rodeo, so let me tell you – us nurses just have to be smart and look out for each other, and we'll get through this just fine.'

Meanwhile, Martha was leaning further and further into the room, straining to hear their conversation. At that moment, the metal door she was leaning on lurched wide open with a loud *creeeeak*. The three women all turned in unison to stare at Martha, frozen in the doorway like she'd been caught with her hand in the cookie jar.

'Who are you?' asked the curly-haired nurse. 'I ain't seen you before.'

Clearly, this woman was the leader of the group. If Martha was going to keep up the deception, she'd have to convince the curly-haired nurse that she was the real deal. She quickly adjusted her posture to be more relaxed, and walked up to where they were standing. Pasting on her brightest smile, she stuck out her hand to the woman and said, 'I'm Martha, from St Louis. Sorry about sneaking around like that – I'm new. I was supposed to be on one of the other hospital boats but they changed my orders at the last minute. I promise I can make myself useful, though,' she added. 'I know French and German, so I can help translate.'

Martha had always found that when lying, it was always best to cling on to as much of the truth as possible. And adding a little sugar always helped people swallow it.

The curly-haired nurse regarded Martha for a moment, one dark eyebrow raised. 'French *and* German, huh? All right, why not,' she said with a sigh. 'Today's already been wilder than an acre of snakes, so what's one more surprise?' She reached out her hand and shook Martha's firmly. 'Welcome to the club, Martha. Can't say it's gonna be fun, but it sure is gonna be one to remember.'

I'm in! Martha thought in triumph.

'The name's Fran, from Corpus Christi,' the nurse continued. 'And that there is Lizzie and Alice – midwestern gals, both. Wouldn't know a chicken-fried steak if it bit them in the rear, but I like 'em anyway.'

Alice rolled her eyes and shook Martha's hand as well. 'Shouldn't be surprised Fran's from Texas,' she chuckled. 'On account of her big mouth.'

Lizzie tried to get up to greet Martha, but before she could even get to her feet she crumpled back onto the bed, holding her stomach. 'I'm sorry, girls, but I think I'm going to be sick,' she moaned.

Martha leaned over to Fran. 'Maybe I could get her topside?' she asked. 'A little fresh air will help.'

Fran nodded. 'Good idea, new girl. She's no use to us like that, anyhow. Alice and I can handle the rest of the inventory here.'

Lizzie continued to moan while Martha dragged her out of the room and climbed the metal stairs to the upper deck. The new day had just dawned, and Martha blinked into the morning light, stained a dusky rose by the sun filtering through the thick grey clouds. The ship's English crew rushed about with their work, while some of the American doctors stood in small groups, talking. 'Did you hear?' she overheard one of the doctors say. 'The first two hospital ships didn't make it to France – hit some mines on the way over.'

'No fooling?' said another, younger-looking doctor.

'No,' the older doctor answered. 'Thankfully, nobody got hurt too bad. But they had to turn back.'

'Gee, do you think we'll make it?'

The older doctor shrugged. 'I hear they cleared out a safe path for us, but I guess we'll just have to see. I hope we do – the boys on those beaches are gonna need us.'

Martha filed that information away for later. *I've got to put some of this down in my notebook when I get the chance*, she thought. *If I get the chance…*

The two women made it to the railing, and Martha stood there with Lizzie's arm still draped across her shoulders, staring out at the dark green water. In times like this, she always liked to focus on the little details. The salty smell of the ocean. The sound of one man whistling a sad song as he kept watch on the horizon. How the giant cans of blood looked, standing in a line along the spotless deck, waiting to serve their grim purpose.

After a moment, she turned to Lizzie, who had her eyes closed and her face turned upward into the wind. She looked decidedly less green. 'You're looking better,' Martha said.

Lizzie opened her eyes and nodded. 'Yes, thank you,' she said, her cheeks reddening. 'A little embarrassed, but otherwise fine. The fresh air really does help.'

Martha chuckled. 'Don't be embarrassed. Fran and Alice may look cool and collected, but they're just as nervous as you are.'

Lizzie shook her head. 'I don't know about that…'

'Well, I do,' Martha replied. 'Fran's foot was tapping the deck like a woodpecker, and Alice must have adjusted her ponytail a dozen times while we were talking. Nervous as heck – both of them. Anyway, it's OK to be scared. It's war. Everybody's scared. Some people are just better at hiding it.'

Lizzie sighed and seemed to relax. She checked her watch and said, 'Well, we should be seeing Normandy on the horizon soon. It's almost time.'

Martha cocked her head. 'Normandy? But I thought the invasion was taking place at Pas de Calais?'

'That's what you were *supposed* to think,' Lizzie said with a sly grin. 'You and everyone else – including the Germans. We didn't find out the truth until this morning when we were briefed. They told us that the Allies had spent months tricking the Nazis into thinking we would attack Pas de Calais, which was the most obvious target, so that they'd be taken by surprise when we invaded Normandy instead.'

Martha was astounded. She thought back on all of the stories she'd worked on in the past year, and all the tight-lipped government officials and military men she'd interviewed, who gave such cryptic answers to her questions that they weren't even worth printing. She'd known something secretive was going on, but she had no idea it was this big.

'Wow!' was all she could manage.

'I'm surprised you didn't get briefed on this,' Lizzie said, a tiny note of suspicion in her voice. 'I thought all the nurses were before we left port.'

Martha kept her face passive. 'Like I said before,' she said with a shrug, 'my orders got changed last-minute – I must have missed it.'

Lizzie looked at her for one tense moment before seeming to accept this and move on.

Whew, Martha thought with relief.

'Anyway, the idea makes sense,' Lizzie continued thoughtfully. 'We tried hitting the French coast at Dieppe two years ago and everyone saw how that went. The Nazis slaughtered us. So, the Allies must have figured if we were going to take back the Western Front, we'd need a better plan. And I guess this was it.'

'It's a good plan, all right,' Martha said, shaking her head in wonder. 'Let's just hope it works.'

'We'll find out soon enough – look,' Lizzie said, pointing. Martha squinted into the distance. Just ahead was an entire floating city of ships. Massive battleships dwarfed destroyers and transport ships, while even tinier vessels flitted through the water like minnows. 'It's the armada!'

Catching wind of this, the American doctors all rushed over to where Martha and Lizzie were standing and crowded around them, leaning out over the railing to see. It was as if every ship in the world had turned out for this mission, a colossal army all of its own. Enormous barrage balloons floated high above the largest ships, making the sky an obstacle course for any enemy planes that dared come near. Beyond the armada, the coast of France lay on the horizon, low and ominous.

'Looks like we made it,' Martha murmured.

Lizzie nodded. 'Looks like we did. And not a minute too late. That landing craft leaving the beach is headed this way, probably carrying wounded,' she added, gesturing at a small vessel speeding towards them. She turned to Martha. 'Are you ready, Martha?'

Martha stared at the scene ahead. In her career as a war correspondent, she'd witnessed violence – terrible violence – and more deaths than she'd like to think about. But what lay before her was like nothing she'd ever faced. 'I don't think anyone is ever ready for something like this,' she admitted. 'But we do it anyway, don't we, Liz?'

'Yes, ma'am,' Lizzie said with a grin. 'We do it anyway.'

At that moment, the captain's voice came over the tannoy and announced, 'All hands to your stations – the first wounded are about to arrive!'

A SEA OF WOUNDED

The hospital ship sailed through the armada, so brilliantly white that it seemed to glow against the dark water and the steel-grey sky. Martha looked and listened, so focused on committing everything to memory that for a minute she forgot to breathe. Their quiet journey across the English Channel soon ended as they got closer to shore, the buzz and clatter of war growing louder by the second. There were the usual sounds of gunshots and explosions, but also the sound of music. Martha craned her neck to catch a glimpse of a small vessel floating nearby, laundry hanging on a line along its starboard deck, dance music playing on its radio. It was a strange, looking-glass world that felt like a dream but was all too real.

For the first time in many hours, Martha thought about Ernest. Was he somewhere nearby, on board one of the many ships spread out all around her? Or had he gone ashore? Was he all right?

She glanced towards the beaches, and watched as the little landing craft came closer and closer. In mere moments, it would reach them.

BOOM!

Martha ducked her head instinctively as a deafening explosion nearby rocked the ship. Mortar shells were falling all around them, but luckily not close enough to hit. After a moment, She stood up again and caught her breath. *Wherever Ernest is right now*, she thought grimly, *I do hope he has his wits about him. I'm certainly going to need all of mine!* Putting on a nurse's uniform was all well and good – but acting as one in the middle of all this was another story! 'You OK, Martha?' Lizzie asked.

'I'm fine, darling,' Martha replied, kicking herself for allowing her feelings to show. 'Just want to do a good job, you know.'

Lizzie nodded. 'Me too. My father fought in France in World War One. It was a miracle that he came back to us in one piece. I really want to make him proud.' She looked back at the incoming landing craft, which was pulling up alongside the hospital ship. 'Time to go. Just follow instructions, help wherever you can, and you'll be fine. OK?'

'Will do,' Martha agreed.

Pushing through the crowd of doctors, the two women ran closer to where the landing craft had anchored. Martha leaned over the railing to get a better look. Dozens of wounded men were lying on stretchers in neat, orderly lines along the deck of the smaller ship, each one covered in a blanket. Some of them bucked and writhed; others didn't move at all. A soldier with a dirt-stained face and a steel helmet stared up at them. 'I've got fifty-plus wounded down here!' he shouted to the hospital ship's crew. 'I need them lifted out on the double!'

A lidless wooden box appeared, and the crew lowered it down to the waiting soldiers using a series of ropes and pulleys. Martha thought it looked like a coffin. In an instant, one of the wounded was loaded into it, and it was hauled back up again in the next. Martha peered over the shoulders of the crewmembers, and saw that the man inside was hardly that – he looked more like a boy. He was as pale as a ghost, and seemed to only have a whisper of life left in him. His uniform was spattered with blood, but even so, Martha could see right away it wasn't the olive green of the American GIs, nor the brown of the British soldiers.

'Ugh, it's one of them Krauts,' one of the crewmembers grunted as he set the box down on the deck.

The older American doctor that Martha had seen earlier stepped in. He was a slight man, with a moustache and round, silver spectacles. 'This German soldier is *dying*, that's what he is,' the doctor said, quickly glancing under the blanket. 'Bullet wounds – two that I can see. Get him to the operating room now!'

The doctor's command seemed to break the final bit of stillness remaining on the hospital ship. The crew and all the medical personnel sprang into action, hauling more and more wounded up from the landing craft. Britons, Americans, Austrians, more Germans – soldiers of all kinds. They laid them out on the deck, sending some straight to the bed ward for care from the nurses, and the unluckier ones for emergency surgery.

Time had crawled by while Martha was in the ship's lavatory, but now, everything seemed to happen all at once. She looked around her, unsure of what to do. Lizzie had been pulled away by one of the doctors to help him start a transfusion on a soldier who'd lost too much blood. Martha was about to follow when she felt something pull her back. She turned to see one of the American soldiers lying in his stretcher on the deck, tugging on her trouser leg. 'Ma'am,' he said politely. His face was blackened with soot, and he held his arm to his chest as if it were broken. Blood seeped from the sleeve of his uniform. 'See that Ranger over there? He's in bad shape.

Could you go to him?' The soldier pointed to another man just across the way, whose tall black boots poked out of the end of his blanket.

Martha nodded silently, and walked over to the wounded Ranger. The top of his head had been wrapped thickly in gauze, covering his eyes. She knelt at his side, and the man's head immediately turned towards the sound of her movement.

'Who's that?' he said, his voice dry.

'It's Martha,' she answered. 'Your friend over there sent me to check on you.'

'Who, Allen? That mud-eater's better off worryin' about himself. Almost got his arm blown off by one of them German chatterboxes.' He chuckled, and then coughed. 'Anyway, I'm all right. Not ready to check out just yet.'

'I'm glad to hear that.'

'And I'm glad to hear *you*,' the Ranger replied, his mouth stretching into a smile. 'Just the sound of your voice sure is a sweet kind of medicine.'

'Can I get you anything?' Martha asked.

'I'd be grateful for some water,' the Ranger replied.

Martha ran to the nearest water tank and returned with a canteen filled to the brim. She helped lift the Ranger's head and tilted the bottle to his lips. He drank greedily, and kept drinking until the canteen was nearly empty. 'Ah,' he said with a sigh. 'Martha, you truly are an angel on earth.'

Martha chuckled, but before she could say another word, two crewmembers came to grab the handles of the stretcher and hoist the Ranger into the air. 'We're taking him down below,' one of them said to Martha. 'There's more wounded incoming, and we've got to make room.'

Nodding, Martha put a hand on the Ranger's arm and said, 'Do me a favour and don't die on me.'

'Roger that, ma'am,' the Ranger replied, before the crew carried him away.

Just then, Martha spotted the captain coming down from the bridge and decided to make her way over to him – it was the first time she'd caught sight of him this whole voyage. He wore a jacket with a fur collar, and a crisp cap with gold embroidery pulled low over his brow. He walked down the stairs with a spring in his step, as if that same dance music she'd heard on the radio was playing in his head. Nothing about the chaos all around seemed to faze him in the least.

Martha stood a few feet away from him at the ship's railing, and together they watched six water ambulances drop off the sides of the hospital ship and float next to it like a brood of little ducklings. 'That beach over there,' a crewman ordered the ambulance helmsmen, 'where they've got two red streamers up. Just this side of Easy Red. *Go!*' The ambulances sped off in that direction without another word, off to collect more wounded. That done, the crew turned its attention to anchoring the hospital ship itself.

'Take her in slow!' came the shouted command. The hospital ship was getting closer to shore now, slipping slowly and carefully into the crowded armada. 'You won't clear any submerged tanks,' another voice shouted. 'So look sharp!'

Floating just under the surface of the water, dark and sinister, the size of small asteroids, were naval mines. *It's a miracle we haven't hit one yet*, Martha thought. The hospital ship edged forwards, ever so slowly, before finally coming to a stop. 'Ready? Lower her!' came the command, and with a rattle that made the whole ship tremble, they dropped anchor.

Next to Martha, the captain crossed his arms and sighed. 'I got us in, all right, but God knows how we'll ever get out.' He waved a hand towards the battleships pressed so close all around them that Martha thought she could reach out and touch one. 'We're squeezed together like a tin of sardines,' the captain went on. 'Well, we'll worry about that later. Won't we, miss…?'

'Martha,' she replied.

'Well, Miss Martha, this your first time in a combat situation?' the captain asked.

'No, sir,' Martha replied.

'Good,' he said, cracking his knuckles. 'Because this ship is no place for rookies. We've jolly well got our work cut out for us today, so be sure to keep your wits about you.'

'Yes, sir,' Martha said with a crisp nod. She glanced towards the beachhead, where troops were unloading from small boats onto a shore clotted with debris. Black anti-tank obstacles lay scattered about, as if a giant had thrown them down for a game of jacks.

The water ambulances returned as quickly as they had gone. They came careening back through the choppy water, brimming over with their cargo of pain. Some of the wounded were still on their feet, crowded close together to make room for those who weren't. The ambulances pulled alongside the ship, and one of the crewmembers yelled, 'We need those stretcher-bearers – now!' The effect was immediate. The crew, the doctors – everyone dropped what they were doing and went to work, lifting and carrying the endless wounded up into the hospital ship.

Martha joined the line, steadying the stretchers wherever she could. Lizzie was there too. Their eyes met, and Lizzie gave Martha a nod, her mouth pressed into a determined line. All traces of her earlier nervousness, Martha noted, were gone.

They went on like that for what seemed like hours, like a bucket brigade trying to put out a fire that never stopped burning. Martha's hands were raw, blisters already forming on her palms. But she barely felt the pain. The adrenaline pumping through her veins made sure of that. Eventually, Lizzie ran up to her and pulled her away from the line. She was red-faced and panting when she said, 'Martha, let the other stretcher-bearers take it from here – they need the nurses down below. Come on!'

Martha swallowed hard. What would she do if they asked her to do a blood transfusion? Or anything else that required medical training that she didn't have?

Look. Listen. Stay calm, she told herself. *An extra pair of hands, skilled or not, are what those boys need right now.*

With that, she took a deep breath and followed Lizzie down into the belly of the ship.

SOLDIERS WITHOUT NAMES

Down below, the clean, empty deck where Martha had first met Lizzie had been transformed into a battlefield, where the doctors were fighting two enemies at once: pain and time. The bunk beds overflowed with men, and the floors were strewn with the remains of the uniforms that had been cut from their bodies, piled next to them like discarded snakeskins. One of the doctors rushed out a door marked 'Operating Room', dressed in a hospital gown and mask. He pushed past her, leaving bloody footprints in his wake.

'They're keeping the worst cases on this deck,' Lizzie told Martha as they walked down the aisle of bunk beds. 'Bullet and shrapnel wounds, severe burns, that kind of thing. Lot of these soldiers are in shock and will need surgery before we get back to England if they're going to survive.'

Martha took in the faces of the men as she walked by. So many of them were still – too still. There was a lieutenant with his entire chest wrapped in bandages, pale and unmoving. He was thin and small, barely more than a child.

'What's his name?' she asked Lizzie.

'Chest Wound?' Lizzie shrugged. 'I don't know. There's no time to learn all their names,' she admitted. 'There's too many.'

Martha had to agree. There were too many.

Another soldier's head was swaddled in bandages, and even so, blood was beginning to seep through in places. Martha could only wonder what his face looked like underneath. Another one was so damaged over the whole of his body that Martha could not imagine how he could live. Next to his bed, she noticed that the tattered uniform piled there was from the German army.

We probably shot the bullets that wounded him, Martha thought. *And now here we are, trying to get them out again*. The thought made her angry and proud and sad, all at the same time.

When they made it to the end of the aisle, Lizzie reached into a crate by the wall and pulled out an armful of fresh bandages. 'Here,' she said to Martha, handing them over. 'Take these down to B-Deck and help with dressing wounds. Fran says they're running low down there. The men on B-Deck aren't as bad off, but they still need to have their wounds cleaned and wrapped with fresh bandages so they don't get infected.'

Martha nodded and turned back the way she came, trying her best not to drop any of the bandages as she went.

But then, just as she passed his bunk, the young man Lizzie had called 'Chest Wound' moved. Martha stopped and watched him slowly prop himself up on one elbow, and look at her with dark haunted eyes. She set the bandages down and knelt next to him. 'Hello,' she said gently. 'Do you need something? Are you in pain?' A tiny red and white tube with a capped syringe on it had been pinned to his bed. *Looks like he's already received a dose of painkillers*, she thought. But who knew what he was feeling? Pain wasn't always just in the body.

Chest Wound didn't answer her. He just stared, and whether he was seeing Martha or some nightmare replaying in his mind, she didn't know. So she just stayed by him, waiting.

Minutes passed. Martha was starting to worry about neglecting her bandaging duties when a quiet, raspy voice reached her ears. 'They wouldn't stop shooting,' the young man said.

Martha moved her head closer to his lips. Obviously, the chest wound had damaged his lungs, and the young lieutenant was struggling to breathe. 'Who wouldn't? The Germans?'

Chest Wound gave a small nod. 'Wounded on the first day. Lay there in a field for hours and hours. Crawled back to our lines but the snipers wouldn't stop shooting. I was already down. But they wouldn't stop. They wouldn't stop.'

Martha said nothing. The lieutenant glanced over and saw a German soldier lying still in the bunk across the aisle. His boyish face twisted with rage, and in a voice barely louder than a whisper he said: 'I'd kill him if I could move.'

He didn't speak again. Martha helped him lie back onto his pillow, picked up her stack of bandages and left, vowing to check on him again later on.

Compared to the grimness of A-Deck, B-Deck was lively and abuzz with chatter. Men sat up in their bunks, talking to each other across the aisle and drinking coffee from tin cups.

One of the men, a blond with a spray of freckles across his face, downed the rest of his coffee and looked up at Martha expectantly. ''Scuse me, ma'am,' he said with a slight southern drawl. 'I sure could use another cup of this.' He winced as he lifted the cup, and Martha noticed his leg bundled at the knee in bloody dressings.

Next to Freckles, a young man with deep brown skin and a small, neat moustache lay in his own bunk, his shoulder wrapped and tied to his chest. 'Maybe some food too?' Moustache asked. He gave her a charming smile and added, 'Pretty please?'

'How about this?' she answered. 'I'll hunt down some stuff for you, if you let me change those dressings without too much fuss.'

Freckles and Moustache both nodded eagerly. 'Much obliged, ma'am,' Freckles said.

Martha ran back up to the top deck and found two young cabin boys wearing bright red jackets. They didn't seem to be doing much of anything, so Martha commanded them to start assembling sandwiches for the wounded. The cabin boys seemed delighted to be given orders, and went to work right away.

A little while later, both Freckles and Moustache had cups of fresh coffee, and were both gobbling up corned-beef sandwiches like they hadn't eaten in a week. As they ate, Martha carefully began unwrapping the field dressing on Freckles' knee. She tried not to show any emotion on her face as she saw the ruin of bone and flesh underneath, and simply did her best to apply the fresh bandage as gently as possible. Most of the men on B-Deck would need surgery too, but since they weren't dying they would have to wait.

Despite his serious injury, Freckles made no complaint as Martha worked. He and Moustache ate, drank and chatted, as if it were just another day in the mess hall.

'Weird, wasn't it?' Moustache was saying. 'You got to that beach, and it's hell on earth. There's screaming and shooting, and it's like the sky is raining fire down on you. Then you get past the beach... and suddenly you're in some kind of fairy-tale village. There's French girls wearing pretty dresses, and offering you flowers and cookies. Heckuva thing.'

Freckles shook his head. 'Ain't that the truth! 'Course it would've been a lot better if we had a translator with us. Couldn't understand a word anybody said.'

Moustache laughed and turned to Martha. 'Listen: So this one villager is talking to us, and we're trying to figure out what she's saying. We think she's inviting us to some lady's house for dinner, so we start to head over. But right before we get there, we realize she didn't say, "*Dame vous a invite à dîner*"; she said, "*Tireurs dans le grenier*."'

Martha's eyes widened as she translated the words. 'Snipers in the attic?'

Moustache smirked. 'Yes, ma'am. Would have been a short meal, don't you think?'

'It certainly would have.'

She finished bandaging up Freckles' knee and turned to Moustache's shoulder.

'Could you do me a favour and check on that boy over there when you're done with me? We're kinda worried about him.' Moustache gestured towards a young boy lying on one of the upper bunks a few beds down. The clothes on the floor next to him were not a soldier's uniform, but the rough brown trousers and white tunic of a farm boy. 'He's from the village. Got tagged in the back with some shrapnel, so I guess they brought him along to fix him up. Got to be scared, not knowing anyone and going alone to a strange country and all.'

Martha promised to do just that, and when she had finished redressing Moustache's shattered shoulder, she walked over to the farm boy's bunk. He was turned on his side away from her, and she could see the bandages wrapped around his body where the shrapnel had hit him. '*Bonjour,*' she said, touching his arm lightly. '*Ça va?*'

The farm boy turned at the sound of his native language, and looked at Martha with grey-blue eyes. '*Êtes-vous infirmière?*'

Martha's years of living in Paris in her twenties had taught her to be quite fluent in French, so it was easy to understand and speak with the boy. She told him that yes, she was a nurse, and asked him if he needed anything. 'Can you tell me what has happened to my family?' he asked in French. 'They are still in the battle. I don't even know if they are alive. Can you tell me how I will get back to them?'

'*Je suis désolée,*' Martha replied sadly. *I'm sorry, I can't.*

The farm boy sighed. '*Alors, non,*' he replied. '*Je ne veux rien de plus.*' *Then no, I don't need anything else.* He set his mouth in a tight line, and said nothing more.

Martha walked back to Freckles and Moustache and reported on what the farm boy had said. Freckles shook his head in wonder. 'That kid's a better soldier than the Kraut in the bunk next to him.'

Just then, one of the ship's officers came onto the deck, making his way over to a doctor examining one of the patients nearby. 'Oi, doc,' the officer said. 'One of the LCTs just came back from Omaha Beach and said that there could still be a hundred or so wounded scattered out there. Starting to get dark, though, so manoeuvring through that mess is going to be tricky. What do you think?'

The doctor's eyes flicked to the porthole, and Martha followed his gaze to the spreading darkness outside. *Night time already?* Martha couldn't believe that so many hours had passed since the wounded starting coming on board in the afternoon. 'Dark or not,' the doctor said, 'we've got to get those wounded off the beach. If the air raids don't kill them, the cold will.'

The officer nodded crisply. 'Yes, sir,' he said. 'We'll send another water ambulance right away. Don't worry, we'll find them.'

Martha watched the officer leave. But before he could even make it out of the room, she had left the bandages on a table for the other nurses to find and trailed along behind him, grabbing up a medic helmet emblazoned with a red cross as she went. Because the moment he'd mentioned another water ambulance heading for Normandy, she'd been seized with an idea.

An irresistible, and completely insane, idea.

She was going with them. She was going to Omaha Beach.

But no one knows you're here, a worried voice in her head reminded her. *If you die out there, you'll die with no one knowing who you really are. You'll die alone.*

But Martha's feet kept moving. They carried her up the stairs, they carried her onto the crowded top deck, and they carried her along with a crew of men onto the small boat rocking in the black, choppy waters.

It'll be fine, she told herself, watching the coast get closer and closer.

In the dark, either no one noticed or no one cared that she was a woman. In the dark, she was just another medic headed for the beach.

7

OMAHA BEACH

'Last stop,' the water ambulance driver shouted, cutting the engine.

From underneath her helmet, Martha squinted into the wind blowing across the water, and glanced out over the shoulders of the men. They were still a good distance from the shore. She gripped the side of the boat tightly as it pitched and rolled on the rough sea. What did he mean, 'last stop'?

'Tide's low and visibility is about as clear as mud,' the driver went on. 'Last thing I want to do is get stranded on that beach. Better make it the rest of the way in on your own, boys. I'll need to look for safe anchorage further down the coast.'

'But what about the wounded?' one of the men asked.

The driver shrugged. 'Do what you can to gather them up. Once the tide comes in, another ambulance will come back for you.'

Martha noticed that they'd pulled up next to an empty cement barge, which she knew the Allies used to help transport troops and equipment closer to shore. One by one, the stretcher-bearers and other crewmembers jumped from the water ambulance to the barge. Martha followed, walking along its length behind the others in a single, quiet line. But the end of the barge was still about sixty yards from shore.

'Hope you're ready for a swim,' one of the stretcher-bearers mumbled to her, and then did a double take when he got a good look at her face. 'Hey! You're one of them nurses – you ain't supposed to be here!'

Uh-oh, Martha thought. *The jig is up.*

It took only seconds for the rest of the men to catch up. 'Lady,' another one said, 'what were you thinking? Don't you know that beach is no place for a woman? You could get killed out there!'

By then, every one of them was looking at her. Martha could see their eyes in the light of the full moon hanging heavy in the night sky. Beyond them, the sounds of faraway gunfire crackled like distant thunder. 'It's true, I could get killed,' she finally said. 'As could all of you. And frankly, I'd like to think I have just as much of a right to get killed defending

my country as you gentlemen do. But we don't have time to quarrel over such things, we've got a job to do.'

The men blinked and looked at each other, unsure of what to do next.

Martha made the decision for them. She jumped off the barge with a terrific splash. The water came up to her waist, and was icy cold. Looking back up to the men, she waved them over with a beaming smile. 'C'mon in, boys, the water's fine!'

There was a pause, and then one of the stretcher-bearers jumped in. The rest quickly followed. Together, they began wading towards the shore, one gruelling step at a time. None of the men made a fuss about her being a woman again.

As the water became shallower, Martha felt the waves pushing her to shore. *Hurry, hurry*, they seemed to say. Her sodden uniform and boots made it difficult to walk, but she forced herself not to slow her pace until she reached land. In the moonlight, the water that splashed up around her ankles looked strange. After a moment she realized it was because it was stained red with blood.

As she and the men came out onto land, it felt as if all the world suddenly went quiet. That first glimpse of Omaha Beach was something Martha never, ever forgot. Decades later, she could still close her eyes and see it all spread out before her: a tapestry of chaos and death.

Ammunition boxes and debris of all kinds littered the beach. There were scores of dead silvery fish too, blasted out of the water by mine explosions and left to suffocate. And all amongst this were the bodies of soldiers.

There were hundreds of them. Maybe more. Some still floated in the shallows, the gentle waves giving them the illusion of movement. Others lay on their backs on the sand, their unseeing eyes open to the sky. Martha's whole body shook, but she forced herself to walk slowly among them. To be a witness. Under the dirt and ash and blood were the faces of fathers, sons, brothers.

She would not look away.

The quiet didn't last long, though. She and the men from the ambulance had no time to mourn the dead. 'Over here!' one of the crewmen shouted, standing near a beached landing ship tank nearby. 'We can collect all the wounded in this LST, and they should be protected until an ambulance comes.' Martha glanced at the canvas roof covering the ship, and thought it wouldn't be protection from very much, but she supposed it was better than nothing. The crewman then gestured towards a tent perched inland on a hill, marked with a red cross. 'Let's check in with the guys up there and see what they've got for us. Careful not to step off the marked path, though. Might be landmines.'

Martha nodded and started to pick her way across to the tent, every step made treacherous by the rocky terrain and the debris scattered everywhere. The ambulance crew walked down a narrow path marked with white tape, making sure not to step outside of it. Up ahead, tanks and trucks rumbled about, and a road shovel dug into the ground like an enormous bomb-sniffing dog. Great clouds of dust rose from the scene, backlit by the grey light of the moon. *It's like the fog of war itself*, Martha thought. She liked the turn of phrase, and tucked it away in the corner of her mind to use whenever she had the chance to write about all this.

Oh! She gasped as her foot slipped on a rock, and she nearly tumbled off the path. Luckily, she caught herself just in time. Her heart hammering, she scolded herself for being distracted and turned all her attention back to getting to the tent. *Focus, Gellhorn*, she thought. *You're never going to be able to write that story if you're blown to smithereens.*

She finally made it to the top of the hill, and took a moment to catch her breath. The air smelled green and sweet with the summer grasses that grew there, which was a welcome change from the choking scent of gunpowder and exhaust. It reminded Martha that this beach had once been a beautiful place. Families had come here to build sandcastles and swim in the ocean. Would it ever be that way again?

She could see a small French village beyond, much of it smashed and smoking. The remains of a quaint little church lay at its centre, collapsed upon itself like a house of cards. She thought of the farm boy on the hospital ship, and silently prayed that his family had managed to survive.

Inside the Red Cross tent were two filthy young men who looked like they hadn't slept in days. 'Good news is, the Allies have taken the beaches,' one of them reported. 'Bad news is, none of our other objectives have been achieved so far. And we've lost a lot of men. Especially here at Omaha Beach.' He told them that they had trucks full of the wounded, and needed to know where to put them.

'There's a covered LST stranded on the beach,' Martha spoke up. 'We were thinking that the wounded would be safe in there until the tide comes in and the ambulances can pick them up.'

The young man seemed surprised to hear a woman's voice issuing commands, and looked to the crewman who'd found the LST in the first place for confirmation.

'She's right,' the crewman said.

'So, we got ladies coming to the front lines now?' the Red Cross man asked.

The crewman shrugged. 'As far as I know, it's just this one.'

'Gentlemen,' Martha broke in, 'may I remind you that there's rather a lot of work to do?'

Her words seemed to break the spell, and once again the group jumped into action. The Red Cross men used their walkie-talkie to tell the truck drivers to deliver the wounded down to the beach, and Martha and the others retraced their steps back the way they came. It took the better part of an hour to carefully transfer the wounded soldiers from the backs of the trucks into the gaping mouth of the landing ship, and everyone was sweaty and tired when it was all done.

Then there was nothing to do but wait, which was somehow worse than the rushing about. Being idle merely gave their minds time to worry about what might come next.

Martha stood at the front of the LST, scribbling down a few things in her little notebook before they vanished from her mind. Eventually some American soldiers wandered over in the darkness and struck up a conversation with her and the other crewmen. They talked about the snipers hiding up in the hills and whether they were from Pittsburgh or Chicago almost in the same breath, as if both things had equal importance. Pretty soon, everyone got to feeling quite comfortable.

'You know,' one of the American soldiers joked, 'I've got a real nice little foxhole just a little way from here. You all are very welcome to come and visit, as long as you don't mind eating sand. Sand's the only thing on the menu at the moment, I'm afraid.'

One of the crewmen chuckled and replied, 'Well, that's mighty kind of you. The thing is, we've got all these guests here in the LST, so I think we've got to stay home for the evening. Maybe another time?'

Martha stifled a laugh, and wondered at how these men could be so jolly at a time like this. *Here we are*, she thought, *stuck in this wretched place with a ship full of dying men. The enemy could shoot us or drop a bomb on us at any moment. And we're laughing? It hardly makes any sense.*

Or maybe it did. *Maybe*, she thought, *when the world is nothing but chaos and horror and you're helpless in the face of it all, maybe there's nothing left to do but laugh.* Whatever it was, she couldn't help but admire the brave, smiling men who grit their teeth and did what they had to do.

Time passed – it might have been one hour or four – and still there was no sign of the water ambulance. It was the darkest part of the night, and Martha could hardly see her hand in front of her face. None of the men dared even to light a match, for fear of the hidden snipers, and so they all just stood there, quietly staring out into the blackness.

Suddenly the silence was shattered by a hollow *boom*. Martha's heart leaped into her throat as, a moment later, an explosion of anti-aircraft flak burst in the sky above them. It was strangely beautiful, twinkling like fireworks, the red tracers glowing brightly as they fell to earth. Despite how pretty it was, though, no one was happy to see it. If the Allies were shooting the big guns, it meant only one thing: there were enemy aircraft flying overhead.

'We've had it now,' one of the stretcher-bearers said grimly.

The nightly air raid had begun.

AIR RAID!

Boom!
Boom boom boom!
Martha watched with growing unease as more flak exploded spectacularly in the darkness above them. 'So,' she said to one of the stretcher-bearers standing next to her. 'What is one meant to do during an air raid?'

The stretcher-bearer, a barrel-chested redhead named Eddie, shrugged. 'Well, if you had the time, you'd find a foxhole to hide in. But there isn't much we can do right here other than watch and pray.'

The jolly soldiers had wandered off to other business, leaving the ambulance crew on their own with the cargo of wounded. Without their good cheer distracting the crew from what was actually happening, Martha and the others became miserable with worry. Not only for the lives of the soldiers in the LST, but for their own.

'I could think of better bomb shelters than this,' Eddie said, eyeing the LST with its thin canvas roof.

'Much better,' Martha agreed. 'And even if we don't get hit, I don't know how much longer these men can last.' She peered into the belly of the ship, where the wounded lay under the weak light of a single bulb. Someone was moaning, but Martha couldn't hear them well enough to understand. The racket was tremendous.

And things only got worse when the anti-aircraft cannon on the LST itself started shooting, firing at an enemy that none of them could see.

'Take cover!' Eddie shouted.

Her pulse racing, Martha crouched down and covered her head with her hands.

Is this the end? she wondered. *Am I going to die here?*

Ack-ack-ack-ack! went the anti-aircraft guns.

The sound inside the steel ship was so loud that Martha felt it in her bones. She thought about her mother, and how upset she would be if she never got the chance to bury her only daughter. She thought of Ernest too. *Will he cry for me?* she wondered. *Will my death end up in the pages of his next book?*

Explosions rocked the world all around them. Someone was screaming.

Will it hurt? Martha thought, fear igniting in her chest like a matchstick. She squeezed her eyes shut, and tried to just keep breathing.

And then... the shooting stopped.

After a moment, Eddie touched her arm and said, 'You OK, ma'am? I think it's done for now.'

Martha's heart slowed as she realized she wasn't going to die – not yet, anyway. *Thank goodness.*

'I'm fine,' she replied, wincing at the continued ringing in her ears. Through the noise, she heard one of the wounded still moaning loudly, his voice desperate. 'But it sounds like someone in there isn't.' Once the ringing in her ears faded, she was able to listen more closely to what the man was saying. The words sounded strange, but it only took Martha a moment to realize why.

Getting up, she walked into the LST among the wounded. They were all dressed in the same kind of olive-green uniforms, with the same silver eagle embroidered on their chests.

'Eddie,' Martha said slowly. 'These wounded... they're all German.'

One of the men reached out to her. '*Bitte,*' he cried. There was blood on his lips. '*Hilf mir. Es schmerzt...*'

'What's he saying?' Eddie asked, seeing the look of understanding on Martha's face.

'"Please help me,"' Martha answered. '"It hurts."'

She bent down close to the soldier. '*Ruhig,*' she said to him. '*Du musst warten.*' Quiet. *You must wait.*

Eddie sighed heavily and put his hands on his hips. 'Well, that is just dandy,' he muttered. 'By golly, if that isn't the pay-off.' After a moment, he added, 'If anything hits this ship, they deserve it.'

'You don't mean that,' Martha said softly. 'More death won't bring back what we've already lost.'

Eddie looked away. 'I don't know,' he said, shaking his head. 'I don't know.'

Martha looked at the wounded Germans. She tried to see them as evil, as heartless villains determined to destroy the freedoms she held dear. But standing there at that moment, all she could see was a bunch of boys, frightened and bleeding in the dark.

She had decided long ago that despite what the leaders of governments said about wars beginning and ending – the truth was that war was a constant. A creature whose hunger would never be satisfied. She hated war with every fibre of her being, and yet, she could not stay away from it. As much as it pained her to see the terrible things she saw, she felt it was her duty to do so.

To see, and then always, to write.

In Martha's mind, there was nothing so important in the world as telling the truth. Hitler and those like him – those who would drag the world into madness – had to be stopped at all costs. Martha knew this. But she was determined to make it known, to everyone, exactly how high those costs were.

'C'mon,' she said to Eddie. 'Let's go topside and see if we can find out what's going on with those ambulances. Any longer and we'll all start speaking French.'

Eddie nodded wordlessly, and they both climbed up a ladder to the upper deck. 'Any news?' Martha asked one of the crewmen keeping watch.

'Nothing yet,' the crewman said. 'Once the tide comes in, this big girl will float, and they'll have an easier time getting to us. Until then…' He shrugged. 'There's coffee in the galley, if you want some.'

'Oh, coffee sounds fine,' Martha said, and followed her nose to the steaming pot inside. She was in the middle of pouring herself a cup when—

Ack-ack-ack-ack!

CRASH!

Martha jumped, and yelped as hot coffee spilled all over her hand. She rushed back outside to see the beach on both sides of the LST engulfed in flames. 'What happened?!' she exclaimed.

Eddie and the other crewman were pumping their fists in delight. 'We got 'em! Took out two of those German bombers!'

Martha stared at the blackened, twisted wreckage of the burning planes, hissing and crackling dangerously. *At least they won't be shooting at us now,* she thought to herself. *At least they didn't crash on top of anyone.*

At least the pilots probably died instantly.

She climbed back down to the wounded, no longer in the mood for coffee. The ones who were still awake made no sound. They just looked at her, and waited.

It was a night that seemed to last years.

The tide trickled in, and eventually the LST lifted off the sand and floated in the water. And as the ship grew lighter, so did everyone's spirits, until finally the water ambulances came back.

'Oi!' came a shout from the dark. 'You mates are in a right two and eight over there, aren't ya?'

From the upper deck, Martha could see a stout little man with a three-day beard shouting at them from the deck of the ambulance. She figured he must be the captain. 'Took you long enough, Bigsby!' one of the crewmen shouted back to him.

'Bah, keep yer knickers on, Tom,' Captain Bigsby growled in a heavy Cockney accent. 'Yer flounder and dab is 'ere. We'll scarper soon enough.'

Jumping into action, Martha helped the other stretcher-bearers load the wounded from the belly of the LST to the ambulance, and with that done, they were on their way back to the hospital ship.

The captain's language only got more colourful as they went, narrowly dodging one obstacle after another in their attempt to reach the ship safely.

'Crikey, mate,' he shouted at one of the drivers, 'wot yer trying ter do, ram a destroyer?' A moment later: 'Keep an eye in yer head, that's a tank radio pole!'

After nearly hitting half a dozen things as they zigged and zagged through the crowded armada, they finally got a clear view of the hospital ship. Her perfect white hull glowed like a moon in the night.

Martha felt faint with relief at the sight of it. The nightmare was over.

9

HOMEWARD BOUND

'Martha! Where in the world have you been?'
Back on board the hospital ship, Martha was helping the stretcher-bearers with the wounded they'd brought back from Omaha Beach, and turned to see Lizzie running up to her. The nurse's eyes narrowed in confusion as she saw that Martha looked as dirty, wet and haggard as the crewmen swarming around her.

'Wait a minute,' Lizzie said. 'You weren't on that ambulance, were you?'

'I was,' Martha replied, pulling off her helmet. She'd developed a splitting headache, and her throat was dry as a bone. Now that the danger had passed, her body begged for food, drink and sleep.

'B-but that ambulance went to the beach!' Lizzie spluttered, following Martha as she shuffled to the canteen. 'You can't tell me you went ashore, Martha!'

Martha filled a tin cup with water and guzzled it all down, letting it dribble down the sides of her mouth and onto her filthy uniform. She wiped her face with her sleeve and turned to Lizzie. 'I'm pretty sure I *can* tell you that, because I did.'

Lizzie's jaw dropped. 'But, Martha, women aren't allowed on the front – you know that!' Her voice dropped to a whisper. 'If any of our superiors find out, you'll be censured, or maybe even thrown out of the Army Nurse Corps!'

They'd have a hard time doing that, Martha thought, *since I'm not actually in it in the first place.*

'I can't imagine what you were thinking,' Lizzie continued, throwing her hands up in the air. 'You'd have to be crazy to get on that boat.'

'I was thinking that the men on that beach needed help,' Martha said, picking out a c-ration, a selection of canned food given to soliders in combat when fresh food wasn't available, from a crate and tearing into the chocolate bar inside. 'And that they probably wouldn't care who was giving it.'

Lizzie regarded her with interest as she gobbled up the chocolate in huge, unladylike bites. 'You really don't seem like a regular nurse, Martha,' she said after a moment, a note of curiosity in her voice.

Martha looked up at her, her unwavering gaze

betraying nothing. 'Look around,' she said. 'Nobody here's regular.'

Outside the canteen, medical teams who'd been working for twelve hours were still bringing up wounded from the ambulances, tirelessly administering medicines, setting bones and pumping blood back into pale, broken bodies. No one stopped. No one complained. At that moment, it didn't matter what country the men came from, or whose side they were on. All that mattered was that the job was done, and done well.

'Guess you're right,' Lizzie murmured.

Martha smiled to herself and swallowed the last bite of her chocolate. The water and sugar had driven her headache away, and she felt a little more like herself again. She might be completely exhausted and aching from head to foot, but she was still Martha Gellhorn, and she could talk her way out of almost anything. 'So, what's next?' she asked.

Lizzie blinked, as if coming out of a dream. 'Oh,' she said. 'Well, the last few hours have been rough – that flak was exploding right above us and it was loud as anything. Didn't bother the medical personnel, but it really spooked the wounded. They're all pretty shell-shocked, I expect. But the ship's heading back to England soon, so we just have to keep them stable till we're home. So far, we've only lost one man, and he came on board a hopeless case. Let's hope it stays that way.'

'All right,' Martha said, nodding. 'Let's go.'

She took her last breath of fresh sea air before heading below. A-Deck, where they were keeping the worst of the wounded, had been half full when she'd visited before, but now every single bunk was occupied. Doctors and nurses filled the aisles, their muttering accompanied by the moans of the wounded who could not sleep. The air was hot and thick, and smelled strongly of coffee, antiseptic and the metallic odour of blood.

It was hard to breathe, but Martha tried to focus on the task at hand. The pathway across the deck was a tangled jungle of hanging plasma bottles and empty food containers, and she picked her way carefully through it, stopping to speak to the men as she passed.

'Is Sergeant Burton here?' one asked. 'He got shot. We tried to bring him with us, but I don't know if he made it…'

'I had a photograph in my jacket,' said another, 'of my girl back home. I can't find it. Where is it? Can you help me find it?'

Another man, whose entire head was swaddled in bandages that covered everything but his nostrils and mouth, quietly asked for coffee.

Martha did her best to address them all in turn, asking after their missing friends, searching inside uniforms for precious items, and pouring coffee into thirsty mouths from the spout of a teapot. Whenever she could, she stole away to jot things down in her notebook – words to capture what it felt like to be there that day.

Sometime later, she collapsed onto a cot in the nurses' quarters and dozed off from pure exhaustion. When she woke again and gazed out the nearest porthole, she could see the pale light of dawn shining through it.

They were heading back to England. The foggy beaches of Normandy, the enemy planes flying overhead, and the great armada had vanished over the horizon. Martha yawned, brushed herself down, and went back to A-Deck to see how the wounded were faring now.

Part of her expected the worst – bodies of men who didn't survive the night shrouded in bedsheets, soldiers growing weaker with every passing hour. But what she found on A-Deck was quite different than that. In the morning light, the men were better.

Miraculously so, in some cases. The young lieutenant they called Chest Wound had undergone surgery overnight and was able to breathe again. She found him propped up in his bed, listening to two of the other soldiers talk. When she asked him what he looked forward to doing most when he got home, he thought for a moment and said, 'Eating a hamburger. With French fries.'

Another man whom she'd believed was far too injured to possibly survive was sitting up drinking coffee. Martha could hardly believe it. The human body was truly an amazing thing. She felt a rush of affection and pride for these marvellous men, and for the doctors and nurses who had worked through the long night to pull them from the jaws of death.

As she walked down the aisles, helping where she could, a teenaged Austrian soldier who'd fought for the Germans stopped her. 'Yes?' she asked.

The young soldier was badly wounded, and winced in pain with every movement he made. '*Bitte,*' he said in German. '*Werde ich jemals wieder nach Hause gehen?*' *Please, will I ever go home again?*

'*Ich weiß es nicht,*' Martha replied. *I don't know.* '*Aber du hast nichts zu befürchten. Du bist hier sicher.*' *But you have nothing to fear. You are safe here.* She gestured at the ocean of wounded – Americans, Englishmen, Germans, French, Austrian and more. Allies, enemies, or civilians: they were all being given the same care.

'*Ja,*' the soldier said, looking at them all. '*So viele Verwundete. Alle wollen nachhause gehen.*' *Yes, so many wounded. Everyone wanting to go home.* A moment later, his face crumpled. '*Warum haben wir mit einader gekämft?*' he cried. *Why have we fought each other?*

Martha's heart squeezed painfully, and she laid a hand on his shoulder. 'There, there,' she whispered, and burned his words deeply into her memory so she would not forget them.

Morning turned into afternoon, and soon the sea air pouring down into the lower decks took on a different scent. It was a green smell – the smell of England. Martha walked over to one of the portholes and looked out. There, in the distance, under the first clear blue sky she'd seen in days, were the yellow beaches of England's coast, beautiful and safe. All around them in the Channel, more ships were making their way towards France to continue the Invasion. The Allies had enjoyed a massive success on D-Day, but Martha knew that the War was still far from over.

On A-Deck, the wounded all seemed to sense that their journey was nearly over. They spoke together with urgency and excitement, and a brightness that matched the sun that shone on their battered faces.

Soon, everyone started bustling about, getting everything and everyone ready to leave the ship. Martha dashed back to the little lavatory and found her old clothes and bag still stuffed in the corner where she'd left them. She rolled them up as tightly as she could and jammed the bundle under her arm before heading topside. *Can't leave any evidence behind*, she thought. She'd managed the entire trip without being caught, so it would be a shame to be found out now.

Up on the top deck, she joined three nurses – Fran, Alice and Lizzie – at the railing. 'Hello, again,' Martha said as she squeezed in next to them. 'Guess we made it through, didn't we, ladies?'

'Guess we did,' Alice replied with a grin.

'What I wouldn't give for a nice cosy bed to sleep in!' Lizzie exclaimed.

All around them the mood on the ship was loud and joyful, as if everyone could hardly believe they'd got back alive. But not Fran. Fran was silent, serious, her ashen-grey face studying the ambulance companies waiting on the docks to sweep up the wounded as soon as they got off the ship. 'You all right, Fran?' Martha asked her after a moment.

Fran looked at her and nodded. She glanced back at the stretcher-bearers, who were starting to carry the wounded up from the lower decks. The walking wounded had begun to emerge as well, stumbling and blinking into the sunlight. 'We did all right, didn't we?' Fran said softly.

'We did more than all right,' Martha replied. 'We did splendidly.'

Fran nodded again, and looked back to England, green and fresh and welcoming. 'We'll do it better next time.'

10

A FLOOD OF WORDS

Within the hour, Martha was in a black cab, on her way back to The Dorchester hotel. Images and sounds and words swirled through her head like a swarm of butterflies, threatening to flutter out of her grasp at any moment. She said nothing to the driver the whole time. She simply closed her eyes and remembered.

Once she was back at the hotel she didn't stop to speak to anyone in the lobby, either. Seeing her walk in, a couple of her journalist friends tried and failed to intercept her.

'Hey, Marty, where you been?'

'You look like something the cat dragged in – what happened?'

But she waved them off, striding to the lifts and taking one up to her room. Inside, she drank a large glass of water, took the hottest shower she could stand, and threw on a dressing gown before plopping down in front of her portable typewriter. She set her little notebook next to her on the desk, battered and still a little damp. She was lucky any of her notes were readable.

She knew that she'd done it all without any accreditation. Knew that all of it – sneaking onto the ship, disguising herself as a nurse, and *especially* going ashore to Omaha Beach – was absurdly illegal. *Collier's* would have every right to take one look at what she was about to write and toss it in the bin.

But Martha was willing to bet that they wouldn't.

Because, illegal or not – this was a story that everyone would want to read, and that no one else had been there to tell.

Martha slipped a piece of paper off the top of the pile on the desk and loaded it into the machine. Some days, the sight of a blank sheet of paper made her queasy – but not that day. It was as if she'd been holding her breath for hours, and the instant her fingertips touched the typewriter keys she could finally let it out. The words poured out onto the pages like water, a flood of memories she'd kept inside since the moment she stepped foot onto the hospital ship.

The United States government had made it pretty clear that they liked it when correspondents like

Martha made the War look good. After all, Americans sacrificed a great deal when they got into World War Two, including the lives of many of their young men and women. Public support of the War was important, and people's opinions were decided by what they saw in the news. Martha understood that as well as anyone. And so when she wrote about the hospital ship, she made sure to include details about the tireless nurses and doctors, the magnificent armada, and the courageous wounded soldiers who defied all odds to survive one of the bloodiest days in American history.

But Martha couldn't just paint a rosy picture and leave it at that. It wasn't what she'd done in the past, and it certainly wasn't going to be what she did now.

People needed to know what war was really like. Not exciting and adventurous like it is in the movies, but full of pain and suffering and terror. She wanted them to know how it sounded there on Omaha Beach, how it smelled, how it felt. She wanted them to see the faces of the dead. She wanted them to feel the weight of it, so they knew what the men who came back were carrying.

The truth. It was Martha's only weapon against injustice. Polished and sharpened, it pierced even the hardest hearts.

The shadows in her hotel room lengthened and vanished as day turned into night. She switched on a little desk lamp with an amber shade, and it filled the room with an orange glow. The words flowed out of her for hours, filling pages that carpeted the floor around her feet, and she stopped neither to eat nor drink until it was done.

Finally, after she pulled the last sheet of paper from the typewriter with a flourish, she gathered them all up into her arms and piled them neatly on the desk. She took a few bites of a stale, two-day old pastry, washed it down with another big glass of water, and collapsed into bed.

The next morning, ignoring the grumbling of her stomach, she immediately went to the press headquarters to clear her piece through the censors. She prayed that her words would be safe from those men's imperious blue pencils and razor blades, which were prone to cut out anything that offended them or gave out too much information about the War. Once they gave the article their blessing, it would be cabled off to *Collier's* in New York.

The question was: would they print her story? Or would they toss her in jail and throw away the key?

Well, it's out of my hands now, she thought with a sigh. Martha could only cross her fingers and hope. Time for a rest – and a meal. She was starving.

Back at The Dorchester, she settled herself at a table in the dining room and ordered a big pot of coffee, eggs, toast and strawberry jam. She was tucking into it all with great zeal when someone walked up to her table.

Ernest.

Her husband looked down at her, a smug grin on his face. His head was still bandaged up from the car accident, and he stood a little crookedly, as if he was favouring one leg. 'Well,' he said, 'I'm sorry to say it, but you missed a real whopper, Marty.'

He didn't sound sorry. Martha swallowed the bite of toast and said, 'Did I?'

'Oh, yes,' he continued. 'I was aboard an attack transport – the *Dorothea M. Dix* – and was instrumental in getting it to Normandy. The ship waged an assault on the beaches in broad daylight. It was stupendous!'

'Didn't get a chance to go ashore, did you?' Martha asked.

Ernest snorted. 'No, but few of us did. Watched the whole thing from the boat – front-row seat, mind you. Anyway, I just sent my transmission off to *Collier's* this morning.'

'That's funny,' Martha said casually. 'So did I.'

Ernest's smile was gone in an instant. 'What are you talking about?' he asked. 'Why were you sending them anything? You have no accreditation.'

Martha shrugged. 'That's true, but I thought *Collier's* might reconsider when they received a story about the first hospital boat to reach Omaha Beach.'

'*What?*' Ernest's face had turned as red as the strawberry jam. 'That's impossible.'

'Is it?' Martha took a delicate bite of her toast and chewed it with great pleasure. She was toying with him, and it made him furious.

'But – but how?'

'Oh, you know me, dear. I always manage to get what I want.'

That was too much for Ernest. He looked like he wanted to overturn the table. But before he could do anything else, a petite woman with curly hair came rushing over to see what all the fuss was about.

'Ernest, is everything all right?' the woman asked.

Ernest seemed to calm down at the sound of her voice. 'Yes, Mary,' he said, turning to her. 'It's fine. Just a little domestic dispute.' He looked back at Martha. 'You remember Mary Welsh, from the *Daily Express*?'

'Of course. Hello, Mary.' Martha kept her expression passive. She knew a rival when she saw one. Ernest was trying to make her jealous, but she simply didn't have the time for all that. The War needed her. Her marriage, or whatever was left of it, would have to wait.

'You should be resting,' Mary told Ernest, patting his arm with affection. 'You won't heal properly if you don't.'

Ernest sighed. 'You're right,' he said. 'Thank you, Mary, for taking such good care of me.' He looked pointedly at Martha, but she simply sipped her coffee.

'Hope you feel better,' she said, and waved as they walked together to the lifts.

Martha finished her breakfast. The food and drink invigorated her, and she decided to gather up all the magazines and newspapers she could find and go back to her room to read and think about her next move.

The Allies would be making their way through France now, fighting to retake the Western Front from the Germans. Pushing the Nazis back to the German border would help immensely in the effort to end the War. But according to the news, there was a lot going on in Italy as well. Two days before D-Day, the Allies had managed to retake Rome, and were moving north through Nazi territory towards Perugia and Florence. If she found a way to get there, she could link up with a unit and write about the Italian front. From the moment the thought entered her mind, Martha knew it was the right decision.

Today, London. Tomorrow, Italy.

She was just thinking about what favours she could call in to get there when there was a knock at the door.

Ernest, she thought with annoyance. *Come to apologize? Or shout at me some more? Maybe brag about his pretty new girlfriend?*

'Listen, Ernest,' she said as she opened the door. 'I don't have time for—'

But it wasn't Ernest. It was another man – three of them, actually – dressed in military uniforms. They seemed to fill up the entire hallway, and beyond them Martha could see curious guests peeping out of their hotel rooms to gawk.

'Are you Martha Gellhorn?' the man in front asked.

'Yes,' Martha said. 'What's going on here?'

'Missus Gellhorn, you are under arrest for illegally crossing to France aboard a military vessel.'

One of the men reached for her wrists and pulled them behind her back before slipping handcuffs onto her. They were cold and sharp against her skin.

Martha paled. 'Can I just—?' she started to say.

'Your article was intercepted by an official at the censor's office,' the first man continued, 'who discovered that you lacked the proper accreditation for the journey. Furthermore, according to your correspondence, you went ashore at Normandy which was also illegal. Women are strictly prohibited from the battlefront.'

Martha said nothing for a moment. 'Wait, does that mean I'm the only woman who made it to the beaches?' she finally asked.

The military officer blinked. 'I mean, I suppose you are.'

Martha beamed. 'Now, isn't that wonderful?'

The officers all looked at each other, confused. 'Ma'am,' the first one said, 'must I remind you that you are *being arrested*?'

'Of course, of course,' Martha said dismissively. They started to lead her down the hallway, but she stopped before they could. Something occurred to her that had suddenly made her sick with worry. 'Just one more thing,' she said. 'Did my story make it to New York? Did they send it?'

The officer sighed. 'The censors found nothing wrong with the correspondence itself, so despite the fact that your actions were illegal, they saw no reason to prevent it from being sent on. It was received and accepted by the magazine a short while ago.'

Martha nodded, relieved. 'Good,' she said. 'That's all I needed to know. Carry on, gentlemen.'

She walked down the hallway with her head held high, and many curious eyes watched her go. *Let them look*, Martha thought. She had no idea what was going to happen to her now – being arrested certainly put a dampener on her plans to get to Italy. But for the moment, she was happy. Her story would soon be in the hands of millions of people, so that they too could know what she knew.

She'd deal with tomorrow – today, she'd won.

A PROMISE

'Ouch…' Martha grumbled, rubbing the back of her neck. She was lying on a hard little cot inside a nurses' training camp, where the military police had taken her after her arrest. Not only had she woken up with a crick in her neck, but a spider had found its way onto her blanket. Again. 'Scram,' she said, flicking the spider away.

Well, it's no Dorchester hotel, she thought. *That's for certain.*

She stared up at the roof of the women's tent, watching it billow slightly in the summer breeze, and thinking about the unfairness of it all.

Three days in this dismal place, she thought. *Three days I could have spent doing something useful, but no. Instead I'm here, punished just for doing my job.* The military police had taken away all of her papers and said she was forbidden to leave the camp.

'Until when?' she'd asked.

'Until we say you can go,' was the reply.

Martha had a terrible feeling that could end up being a long, long time.

The other women buzzed busily around her as they went about their morning rituals and duties, giving Martha a wide berth. A couple of the girls had tried to befriend Martha when she appeared that first day, asking if she was a nurse as well.

'I'm not a nurse, I'm a criminal. See?' Martha tilted her head towards the officer who stood guard at the entrance to the tent. 'This might be a fun little jaunt for you girls,' Martha went on, dropping her bag unceremoniously onto the cot. 'But for me, it's prison.'

The young nurses' eyes had widened at that. 'Oh!' they'd said, and skittered away to whisper to each other on the other side of the tent. Everyone pretty much left Martha alone after that.

Martha got up, washed her face and got dressed, taking care to brush and style her hair. They could take her accreditation, her ration entitlements, and even her freedom – but she wouldn't let them take her pride. That done, she walked out past the guard for her morning walk around the perimeter. The grassy earth was soft beneath her feet, soaked through after a rain shower overnight. A tall wire fence enclosed the women's tent and the other temporary structures of the camp, and beyond that she could see the rolling green hills of the countryside, as well as a small village in the distance. She was somewhere in the no-man's-land outside London, far from the front lines.

Too far, she thought.

The adrenaline she'd felt after her adventure on the hospital ship had faded, leaving Martha feeling restless and annoyed. Being in that camp made her feel like a caged animal, and she was desperate to get out and find a way to return to the battlefront. But how?

She was so distracted by the question that she almost tripped over a rock in her path. Kicking it out of her way, Martha watched as it rolled out of view near the perimeter fence. Curious, she walked closer and pushed the tall grass aside, revealing a dip in the ground she hadn't noticed before. The rock had rolled right under it, below the fence. Martha reached her hand down into it, and realized that the depression went all the way out to the other side.

Hmm.

It would be a pretty tight squeeze, but maybe, just maybe…

That night, Martha waited until everyone was asleep and quietly rose from her cot. It must have been after midnight, and the guard had nodded off in his chair at the entrance to the tent. Martha slung her packed bag over her shoulder and snuck past him, making a beeline for the hidden spot in the fence.

She shoved her bag underneath first, then lay down on the grass on her belly. It was wet with dew, and soaked through her clothes almost instantly. Gritting her teeth, she rolled down into the depression. The sharp points of the wire fence snagged her coat and hair, but she kept pushing through. Seconds later, she was on the other side, ragged and breathless, her clothing torn in several places. She was most likely bleeding from somewhere or another, but she was free.

Thought you could keep me in a cage, eh? Martha thought, a smug smile spreading across her face. *Nice try, fellas.* She was officially AWOL – absent without leave. They'd already threatened to deport her back to the United States if she tried to get away.

Well, they'd have to catch her first.

The camp on the other side of the fence was quiet. Martha took one last look at it before starting the long hike to the village beyond.

After walking for a couple hours through the night, Martha made it to the tiny village station and caught the first train back into London. It was still early morning when she marched back into the lobby of The Dorchester hotel, to the total shock of the attendant at the front desk, who'd seen her taken away in handcuffs just days before.

'Um,' he started to say as she passed.

'Don't ask,' Martha grumbled.

'As you wish, Missus Gellhorn,' he said, handing over her room key without another word.

Martha went back up to her room. She'd left most of her things there, and her typewriter sat on the desk, quietly waiting. Sitting down, she typed up two letters – a cheerful one to her mother back in St. Louis, reassuring her that everything was fine and that she was having a whopping good time reporting on the War; and a stern one to Colonel Lawrence in the American army, informing him of the unacceptable way that female war correspondents were being treated. They might be angry once they discovered her escape from the training camp, but she was going to make sure they knew that she was pretty angry too.

She slid the letters into envelopes, spritzing her mother's with a little perfume as she did so. Perhaps she'd bent the truth a little in that letter, for the real picture wasn't nearly as rosy. Everything was *not* fine, but she didn't want her mother to worry. She tucked the envelopes into her bag, thinking she would post them on her way out. She'd decided to go out to eat – she'd rather not have to answer any questions from curious reporters or hotel guests.

After a quick wash and changing her clothes, Martha left The Dorchester and found a cafe nearby. A dozen or so people sat inside, filling the air with morning chatter and the clinking of cutlery. She took a table at the back, so she could watch people coming in and out, and ordered tea and a pastry. Sipping her drink, she spread the morning's newspaper out on the table and scanned the headlines.

A little while later, a couple of young military men walked in and sat at a table nearby, ordering plates of toast and jam. They wore the crisp, navy-blue uniforms of Britain's Royal Air Force, and placed their caps on their knees as they ate. One of them was tall and thin, with a face like a razor blade, and the other was shorter and gentler looking, with watery blue eyes. Keeping her eyes on the newspaper, Martha did her best to eavesdrop on the conversation.

'We took Rome all right,' the taller pilot was saying. 'But the German Tenth got away, and now we're paying for it. It's going to be a tough go, getting to the Gothic Line with that damned Nazi army jamming up the works.'

The shorter one nodded. 'Especially now that they're pulling those seven French divisions back to the Western Front. Anyway, my orders are to fly back to Naples tomorrow, so I guess I'll be in the thick of it with the rest of our lot pretty soon.'

Martha sat up straight, as if electrified. *Hah! He's flying to Italy tomorrow*, she thought. *What he doesn't know yet is that I'm flying with him!*

Within moments, she had concocted a plan. It was time for a show.

'Excuse me, gentlemen,' she said softly. She got up from her table and approached them, her hands fidgeting at her sides. 'I'm sorry to bother you, but I couldn't help but overhear you say that you're going to Naples tomorrow.'

'Yes… ?' the shorter one said warily.

'Shouldn't be listening in on conversations during wartime, ma'am,' the taller one scolded. 'Loose lips sink ships.'

Martha took that golden opportunity to burst into fake tears. 'I'm so sorry!' she wailed. 'I shouldn't have, but I'm desperate – desperate to get to Italy!'

The shorter man seemed bewildered by Martha's sudden outburst, and immediately jumped to his feet to pull out a chair for her. 'Madam, please, uh, sit,' he stammered. 'Calm down, now. Just tell us what's wrong. My name is Roger. Why do you need to get to Italy?'

Martha sniffled and dabbed her eyes with a napkin. 'My fiancé is there,' she said. 'He's a soldier in the American Infantry. We were about to be married when he was called away. I got word two weeks ago that he's fallen ill. Malaria. I have got to be with him, do you understand? I've come such a long way…' She started to sob.

'Oh, no, no,' Roger said, wringing his hands. 'No more tears. If you want a ride, I don't see why I couldn't slip you onto my plane. No one has to know—'

'Roger!' the taller pilot exclaimed. 'You don't even know her name!'

'There's a war on, mate,' Roger replied. 'We've all got to help each other out in times like this. And I know a good woman when I see one. Just keep your mouth shut, and no one will be the wiser. Isn't that right, madam?'

'My lips are sealed,' Martha said, squeezing the pilot's hand. 'Thank you, officer. You've saved my life today.'

Roger beamed.

Martha closed her eyes, a sense of relief washing over her. The story she'd cooked up was a lie, but the last part was true. Roger the pilot *had* saved her life today. Because of him, her war work wouldn't end here in London. Maybe it wouldn't end at all.

Twenty-four hours later, Martha and her typewriter were strapped into the bomb bay of Roger's de Havilland Mosquito fighter plane. She'd checked out of The Dorchester that morning, leaving a note for Ernest at the front desk.

Darling, it said. *I'm off again. To where, you needn't know. I love you, that's the main thing. It may not be enough any more, but for what it's worth, I do. Until we meet again.*
    Sincerely,
        Marty

            P.S. Don't do anything stupid.

At the front of the plane, Roger and his navigator went through their pre-flight routine, checking dials and flipping switches as the engine rumbled like a lion.

'Ready for take-off.'

Martha gripped the seat under her tightly as they sped down the runway. When the plane took flight, she felt her heart lift and her breath catch. To fly was to defy gravity, to do the impossible. It spoke to her, that feeling. It was what she always aimed to do in her life. '*To strive,*' as the poet Tennyson once wrote, '*to seek, to find, and not to yield.*'

She had no idea what was waiting for her in Italy. Sorrow, most likely. And courage. It would make her angry. But it would also give her the fuel to keep going.

Peering out the front of the plane, she watched the English countryside fall away, replaced with only sky.

She pulled out her little notebook, and wrote these words inside it: *No matter what happens, I will follow the War wherever I can reach it.*

It was a promise. To herself – and to the world.

She never broke it.

WHAT HAPPENED NEXT...

THE MANY ADVENTURES OF MARTHA GELLHORN

The story of Martha Gellhorn talking her way onto a hospital ship during the D-Day invasion may be the most well-known story about Martha, but in reality, it is only one of the many amazing adventures she experienced throughout her incredible life. Martha was famously busy in seeking out the truth and reporting on it.

This short *True Adventures* story doesn't have room to include everything Martha did in London before embarking on that hospital ship. In fact, she spent a whole day – D-Day itself – talking to people around London, and frantically trying to figure out how to get to France before making her way to the ports. And after she escaped from the nurses' training camp, she spent quite some time in London – visiting people like author H.G. Wells – before making her way to

Naples to cover the advance of the American troops through Italy. Then, for the next year until the War ended, Martha travelled across Europe, continuing to report on the War for *Collier's*, and defying the military's punishment for her actions during D-Day.

But Martha didn't stop once World War Two was over. After her divorce from Ernest Hemingway, she went on to report on the continuing war in Java – an island in Indonesia – as well as the Nuremberg Trials and the Paris Peace Conference in 1946. The Nuremberg Trials were set up to establish the guilt and then punish Nazi leaders for war crimes and crimes against humanity, which gave Martha hope that the atrocities of the War would not be repeated. The Peace Conference, however, only made Martha worry that her wishes for a peaceful future would not come true.

Unfortunately, war continued to break out across the world as time went on. In 1966, Martha spent time reporting on the United States' conflict in Vietnam, which she saw as a new and terrible kind of war. She wrote six articles about it, focusing on the plight of the Vietnamese people – particularly the children. In 1967, she travelled to Israel to write about the Six-Day War, the shortest one she ever covered. Her reports spanning all these conflicts clearly demonstrated that Martha wasn't interested in anything but the truth – no matter how ugly it might be. She never backed down from criticizing leaders and governments around the world for what she saw as corruption, greed or cowardice.

After covering the war in Nicaragua in the early 1980s and the United States' invasion of Panama in 1989, Martha finally decided she was 'too old' for war, and retired from journalism. She died in 1998 after a long illness, leaving behind her adopted son, Sandy.

As the first officially recognized female war correspondent, Martha Gellhorn left an unforgettable mark on the world. For more than fifty years, she followed wars wherever they led her, and ran into the face of danger again and again in pursuit of truth and justice. 'If nobody puts it down on the record,' she once said, 'then the monsters win totally.' In honour of her service to humanity, the Martha Gellhorn Prize for Journalism was established in 1999, and is awarded every year to a journalist whose work demonstrates the same kind of courage that Martha showed throughout her career.

TIMELINE

1934   Chancellor Adolf Hitler becomes absolute dictator – or *Führer* – of Germany, dismantling the last remnants of the country's democratic government and making way for the establishment of the Nazi party.

1937   Martha Gellhorn begins her career as a war correspondent during the Spanish Civil War, which she always believed was a prelude to the coming battle between dictatorship and democracy throughout the world.

1939   Hitler invades Poland, causing its allies – France and Great Britain – to declare war against Nazi Germany and mark the beginning of World War Two.

1940   Countries around the world join the fight on both sides. The Battle of Britain, which destroyed parts of London and many other towns and cities across the Commonwealth, begins. France falls to Germany.

1941   Japanese warplanes attack the US fleet in Pearl Harbor, Hawaii. After remaining out of the fight for three years, the United States declares war on Japan and joins the Allied Forces.

1942	Germany kills millions of Jews, political opponents and other innocents in concentration camps across Poland, marking the height of the Holocaust. Unable to get a commission from the US military to report on the War – due to being a woman – Martha Gellhorn begins work on her novel *Liana*.
1943	War continues to rage on multiple fronts: in Europe, in Africa and the Middle East, and in East Asia. Martha Gellhorn arrives in London to finally report on the War for *Collier's*, her husband Ernest Hemingway having elected to stay behind in Cuba.
1944	The Allies invade German-controlled France on D-Day, landing in a surprise attack on the beaches of Normandy. After a brief stint back in Cuba, Martha Gellhorn returns just in time to witness and write about the historic event, despite no longer having her accreditation. Between 1938 and 1944, *Collier's* publishes twenty-six of her articles.
1945	Martha Gellhorn continues to cover the War across Europe. Germany surrenders to the Allies after Hitler's death. Japan surrenders as well after the United States drops atomic bombs on two major cities. By September, the War is over.

A LITTLE MORE ABOUT MARTHA GELLHORN'S WORLD

ALLIED FORCES & AXIS POWERS

There were two groups of countries who fought against each other during World War Two. The Allied Forces were made up of the 'Big Four' – the United Kingdom, the United States, the Soviet Union and China – as well as more than a dozen other nations across the world. The Allies fought against the aggression of the three countries that made up the Axis Powers: Germany, Japan and Italy.

ANTI-AIRCRAFT WARFARE (ACK-ACK)

These land-based weapons were used to fight back against attacks from the air. Fire coming from anti-aircraft guns or cannons was often called 'flak'.

BARRAGE BALLOONS

These blimp-shaped balloons, held in the air by steel cables, were used in both World War One and Two as airborne obstacles. Barrage balloons made it very difficult for enemy aircraft to fly unimpeded and drop bombs over cites and military fleets.

CHATTERBOX

This was soldiers' slang for 'machine gun'.

CUBA

This is an island country located in the Caribbean, roughly ninety miles south of Florida. Martha Gellhorn and her then-husband, Ernest Hemingway, bought a house there called the *Finca Vigia*, and lived there for the majority of their marriage. Both Martha and Ernest wrote many of their novels in Cuba, and were famous for keeping a large number of polydactyl cats as pets at their home.

D-DAY

This was the day that the Allied Forces invaded the German-occupied beaches of Normandy, France. By tricking the Nazis into believing that they were attacking a different location at Pas de Calais, the

Allies were able to take Normandy back and continue to push the German army back through France and Western Europe. D-Day marked the largest seaborne invasion in history.

ERNEST HEMINGWAY

Thought to be one of the greatest American writers of the twentieth century, he wrote such classics as *A Farewell to Arms*, *The Sun Also Rises*, and *The Old Man and the Sea*. Martha Gellhorn herself is credited for inspiring him to write his most famous novel, *For Whom the Bell Tolls*.

LST (LANDING SHIP TANK)

These ships were developed in World War Two to carry tanks, vehicles, cargo and troops across waterways and deliver them onto beaches.

NAVAL MINES AND LANDMINES

These are explosive devices used in wartime to destroy enemy vessels, vehicles and personnel. Naval mines, which can weigh hundreds or even thousands of pounds, are placed underwater and are triggered by contact with ships or submarines. Landmines are much smaller, and are hidden in the ground and triggered by a target stepping on it or driving over it.

NAZIS (NATIONAL SOCIALIST PARTY)

This was a political group in Germany, originating in the 1920s, led by Adolf Hitler. The Nazis believed that they were a superior people who had the right to dominate and destroy other people whom they saw as inferior to them. The Nazis' rise to power directly led to the beginning of World War Two.

OMAHA BEACH

This was the codename for one of the five Normandy beaches invaded by the Allied Forces on D-Day. The coastline was broken up into six sections: Dog Green, Dog White, Dog Red, Easy Green, Easy Red and Fox Green. Omaha Beach represented the most famously challenging battle of the day, and where the Allies suffered the heaviest loss of life.

OPERATION OVERLORD

This was the codename for the Allied Forces' plan to retake France and Western Europe from Nazi control in 1944. The operation was kept top-secret for an entire year, with Allied spies and resistance fighters used to sabotage German efforts and plant false information.

THE RED CROSS

This is an international movement dedicated to protect human life and health, and ease human suffering. During World War Two, the Red Cross worked in camps for Prisoners of War (POWs), provided relief for civilian populations in war zones, and helped with exchanging messages about prisoners and missing persons.

WAR CORRESPONDENT

This is a journalist who travels to war zones to observe and report on events at the battlefront.

INCREDIBLE PEOPLE
DOING INCREDIBLE THINGS

The most thrilling stories in history

THE KINGDOM OF JHANSI. 1857.

The British first came to India as traders. Now they're here as soldiers, taking over new territories, and they've got their eye on the small kingdom of Jhansi. But they aren't prepared for the kingdom's courageous queen. Lakshmibai, the Rani of Jhansi, is determined that the kingdom will pass from her to her adopted son.

So when the British demand that she hand over control, she refuses. And when an uprising begins to stir, the Rani will have to decide whether or not to join the fight.

THE AMERICAN CIVIL WAR. 1863.

On a cold beach in South Carolina, the soldiers of the 54th Massachusetts Regiment are marching into battle. Their mission: to capture the impregnable Fort Wagner. The stakes could not be higher – they are one of the first all-Black regiments in the Union Army, and all of America is watching them.

Among their ranks is William Harvey Carney. A former enslaved man who escaped to the North, he knows what a precious thing freedom is. So when the bugle sounds, and the regimental flag is hoisted high, William charges towards the guns.

JOHANNESBURG. MARCH 1961.

Thirty-one activists are on trial for treason. Among their numbers is Nelson Mandela, a rising star of the resistance movement and one of the biggest threats to the South African government and their racist system of apartheid. Along with the other activists, he is found not guilty. But rather than relish his newfound freedom, Nelson disappears. For months, he was an outlaw, hunted in vain by the police and the secret services, living under new identities and in various disguises, separated from his young family. His mission? To set up armed resistance to apartheid.